What They're Saying

"A superb resource for entrepreneurs that provides smart, actionable tips and advice for getting nearly any business off the ground—and successfully keeping it running."

Barbara Corcoran
Real Estate Mogul
Star of ABC's *Shark Tank*

"*The Business Expert's Guidebook* offers amazingly helpful advice in digestible bites—and combines practical, experience-based knowledge with up-to-date technical savvy. It's the one book every entrepreneur should keep handy."

Gary Shapiro
CEO, Consumer Electronics Association
Author, *The Comeback: How Innovation will Restore the American Dream*

"At the same time encyclopedic and amazingly compact: An extraordinary resource for any start-up or well-established business."

Dick Bolles
Author, *What Color Is Your Parachute 2012*

"Unbelievably packed with practical, useful and valuable advice."

John Jantsch
Author of *Duct Tape Marketing*

"A great resource for entrepreneurs who are looking to use cutting-edge technology to grow their business."

Dan Schawbel
Founder, Millennial Branding
Author, *Me 2.0: 4 Steps to Building Your Future*

"A must-have... Don't start a business without it!"

Anita Campbell
CEO and Publisher, Small Business Trends

"A *CliffsNotes* for any small business or startup that offers practical advice for marketing, social media, and maximizing the opportunities that technology can bring."

Thomas Byun
VP and General Manager, Yahoo! Small Business

STRATEGIC CONSULTING | PRODUCT TESTING | MARKET RESEARCH | EXPERT WITNESSES

www.TechSavvyGlobal.com

As Seen On:

ADDITIONAL RESOURCES:

BUSINESS
EXPERT
SMALL BUSINESS TIPS, TRENDS AND ADVICE

SMALL BUSINESS TIPS, TRENDS AND REVIEWS
VIDEOS AND ONLINE TRAINING

www.ASmallBusinessExpert.com

SOCIAL MEDIA **EXPERT**
S E R I E S
www.ASocialMediaExpert.com

SOCIAL MEDIA CONSULTANTS:
FACEBOOK, TWITTER, GOOGLE+ (PLUS), YOUTUBE AND MORE

www.ASocialMediaExpert.com

WORK I LIFE I PLAY > CONNECTED

WORK, LIFE AND FAMILY TIPS
PRODUCT NEWS, REVIEWS AND TRENDS

www.TechSavvyMag.com

Published By:

A NEW CHAPTER IN HIGH-TECH PUBLISHING

WRITERS WANTED

FOR TECHNOLOGY AND BUSINESS BOOKS

www.BooksAboutTechnology.com

THE
Crowdfunding
B I B L E

HOW TO RAISE MONEY FOR ANY
STARTUP, VIDEO GAME, OR PROJECT

By
SCOTT STEINBERG
with RUSEL DeMARIA

Edited by JON KIMMICH

Download FREE Now

EDUCATE. ELEVATE. EMPOWER. ENTERTAIN.™

FROM SMARTPHONES AND APPS TO TABLET PCS AND SOCIAL NETWORKS, TECHNOLOGY has changed everything for today's business owner—small or otherwise.

Credit an increasingly connected and globalized workforce that's capable of staying competitive virtually anytime, anywhere, thanks to the rise of mobile devices and cloud computing. But just as advancements such as Web applications and social media, search engine optimization (SEO) and online commerce continue to transform the field, some things remain the same. As ever, for resourceful entrepreneurs, startups and small business owners, it's all about the bottom line – increasing ROI, maximizing revenue and boosting productivity without sacrificing performance, quality or customer service.

Designed for a new breed of tech-savvy entrepreneurs and startups, *The Business Expert's Guidebook* series reveals how to make technology work for you. As equally accessible to small business owners as large enterprises and home business providers, volumes are specifically designed to address the modern executive's needs. Covering a complete range of topics from leadership and management to advertising, marketing and public relations, each illustrates how to slash costs and improve efficiency by incorporating today's best practices and latest high-tech innovations.

Like companion video series *Business Expert: Small Business Tips, Trends and Advice*, all provide news, reviews and step-by-step guides that demonstrate how to put the hottest new apps, gadgets and software to work. Offering direct and actionable strategies that can help you kick-start sales, enhance customer relations and fuel enterprise growth, each book offers simple, cost-effective solutions and resources that benefit your business. Created by entrepreneurs for entrepreneurs, and featuring insights and input from top industry leaders, be sure to tune in today.

As the world's most successful companies and brands already know, like hardware, software and applications, every business – and business plan – can profit from keeping up with the hottest new IT advances. Join us as we reveal how to give yours an upgrade.

Scott Steinberg
www.ASmallBusinessExpert.com

THE BUSINESS EXPERT'S GUIDEBOOK

SMALL BUSINESS TIPS
TECHNOLOGY TRENDS
ONLINE MARKETING

SCOTT STEINBERG

THE BUSINESS EXPERT'S GUIDEBOOK
SMALL BUSINESS TIPS
TECHNOLOGY TRENDS
ONLINE MARKETING

DEDICATION

For R, K, J, L, Z, K and V, who never doubted, even when the phone didn't ring.

For Florence de Martino, Elliot and Olivier Grassiano, Mark Fusco, Nolan Bushnell, Bjorn Larsson, Trip Hawkins, N. Paul, David Perry, Nathaniel Hale, Paul Scigliano, Ted Nathan, Eric Knipp, Josh Humphries, Richard Fliehr, THG, Terry Bollea and Todd Anthony Shaw – inspirations all.

But most of all, for everyone who's ever wondered: Opportunity always knocks – all you have to do is listen.

Foreword XIV

Introduction XVI

PART 1: MARKETING
BUILDING YOUR BRAND

Chapter 1 – What Makes You So Special? Building Your Personal Brand **2**

Chapter 2 – Self-Publishing Solutions: How to Start a Business Overnight **8**

Chapter 3 – Make Your Brand Pop: Today's Hottest High-Tech Marketing Trends . . **17**

Chapter 4 – Top Online Marketing Strategies **21**

Chapter 5 – Crowdsourcing and Minimum Viable Product: Marketing in Action **26**

Chapter 6 – Sales and Business Development: The Inside Secrets **34**

Chapter 7 – Lessons from Guitar Hero: Marketing Mistakes to Avoid **40**

PART 2: PUBLIC RELATIONS
LEVERAGING THE POWER OF PRESS
AND SOCIAL MEDIA

Chapter 8 – Power PR: How to Make Headlines **44**

Chapter 9 – Working with the Media: Cultivate a Winning Public Image **49**

Chapter 10 – Using Twitter to Boost Your Business **55**

Chapter 11 – Building an Online Community: 10 Tips for Success **61**

Chapter 12 – Individual PR: Promoting a Self-Published Book **65**

PART 3: TECHNOLOGY
IT AND MOBILE SOLUTIONS

Chapter 13 – Recent Technology Trends: Leading the Way in Business Devices . . . **70**

Chapter 14 – High-Tech Services and Gadgets: Great Money Savers **74**

Chapter 15 – Save More Money: Best Free and Low-Cost Software Solutions **76**

Chapter 16 – Must-Have Gadgets for Business Owners **79**

Chapter 17 – Ultrabooks: Should You Buy One? **85**

Chapter 18 – Go-Go Gadgets: Mobile Devices and Technologies **87**

Chapter 19 – Best Business Smartphones and Buying Tips **89**

Chapter 20 – All About Apps: Best Business Apps for Smartphones and Tablets . . . **93**

Chapter 21 – 5 Ways the iPad Benefits Business **97**

Chapter 22 – 10 Tips for Online and High-Tech Security **101**

Chapter 23 – Storage Solutions: Protect Data from Catastrophic Failure **104**

Chapter 24 – Protecting Your Business from Identity Theft **107**

Chapter 25 – 7 Ways to Make Your Small Business Look Big **110**

Chapter 26 – 8 Reasons to Fire Your Personal Assistant **112**

F O R E W O R D

S TARTING AND GROWING A BUSINESS IS EASIER, CHEAPER AND FASTER THAN EVER before, largely thanks to the nonstop proliferation of low or no-cost Web-based tools, apps, software and gadgetry available to business owners worldwide. Coupled with the unprecedented rise of globalization and automation, business today looks very different than it did even a decade ago.

Just think: When the iPhone first hit the market, none of us imagined how much it would alter communication and business as we knew it. It's certainly changed the way I operate. As founder of the Young Entrepreneur Council, a nonprofit, invite-only membership organization comprised of several hundred of the world's top young entrepreneurs, I'm on the road a lot, and that means time (and contacts) are of the essence. Without my smartphone, I would still be tethered to a desk somewhere.

But today, business happens everywhere. During the year and a half since the YEC was founded, I've witnessed firsthand the fact that business technology, and the data it provides us with, is no longer the esoteric realm of developers and programmers alone. Nor do the basics require a massive financial investment, as I tell aspiring young entrepreneurs every day. From collaborating with a remote team to building a clean and simple WordPress website using talent sourced on a site like oDesk or Elance, it takes little more than a few hundred bucks to start building a viable brand that impresses, motivates and inspires prospective customers.

Case in point: The YEC. In November 2010, the organization started as an informal listserv – and quickly grew, in a little over a year, to become the most widely syndicated entrepreneurship content provider on the globe. But without Facebook, Twitter, WordPress, Google, Dropbox, Basecamp, and the (often virtual) talent to manage them all, our growth thus far – including mentoring 10,000 young entrepreneurs, being honored by the White House and NASDAQ, and launching a nationwide campaign against youth unemployoment called #FixYoungAmerica – would probably be unthinkable. At a minimum, our achievements would have taken us twice as long and carried an unsustainable price tag. It truly is an incredible time to do business, at the startup or enterprise level.

Yet all this technology can quickly become a double-edged sword for business leaders trying to cut through the noise, slash overhead costs and stand out. All of this technology is worthless if you can't execute, drive sales and grow. And that's where The Business Expert's Guidebook comes in: It provides an invaluable roadmap for becoming a more resourceful and connected leader, including one who leverages new IT resources to automate and delegate. Whether you're starting a new business or are tasked with growing a department, this book is an up-to-date, comprehensive and actionable resource for any leader looking to work better – and smarter – in 2012 and beyond.

–Scott Gerber, Founder, **Young Entrepreneur Council**

MANY PEOPLE LIKE TO ROMANTICIZE ENTREPRENEURSHIP. AS EXPERIENCED SMALL business owners know though, the day-to-day reality of running any enterprise is hardly the stuff of which reality TV is made. More often than not, the average workweek is either an all-out sprint, emotional rollercoaster ride or heart-wrenching exercise in problem-solving and persistence – sometimes all of the above. But therein lies the almost mystical appeal that continues to captivate millions, as reflected in countless rags-to-riches tales of scrappy underdogs chasing the American Dream, and the funhouse mirror of popular shows such as *Shark Tank* and *The Apprentice*.

Don't let Donald Trump or Richard Branson fool you, however: Few become self-made billionaires, and charting a haphazard course through the constantly-shifting commercial environment is a task that's nothing short of Sisyphean. Still, creating a company from scratch, then plotting a strategic roadmap to success come hell or high water, can be one of life's most uplifting and rewarding endeavors. Be forewarned, though, if you do decide to take the plunge – a wise man once equated the process of incubating and stewarding startups to playing football. You'll fight tooth and nail to gain precious ground by the inch, only to then be brutally mauled and ridiculed by armchair quarterbacks when you're forced to cede hard-won advancements just seconds later. Resourcefulness and heart are what separate the winners from losers in this grudge match, though: Success is often simply a function of how many times you're willing to pick yourself up, brush off the dirt and get back in the game. Some days you gain yards, others lose them. Ultimately, all that matters is keeping the ball moving downfield in the aggregate.

But having to endure such hardships, and triumph in the face of overwhelming odds, is also the attraction. True entrepreneurs don't spend their days idly daydreaming about hogging the spotlight or securing early retirement. Instead, they simply lace up their shoes, put on their poker face and steel themselves to greet each and every day, because they know it's war out there in the trenches. Such individuals will, at some point in their career, undoubtedly be tempted by the prospect of wealth, power and fame, as would any working professional. But in the end, most are driven by other, more inborn factors.

For some, it's the thrill of being their own boss. Others will find that they relish the magic of birthing new and original ideas into the world. Still more will discover that their greatest personal rewards come from building a brand from nothing to something through the fruits of their own labor. Regardless of whether you're motivated from a simple desire to set your own working hours, or compelled to find meaning in life by shedding blood, sweat and tears in pursuit of an elusive dream, make no mistake, though. Near universally, no matter the individual's background or the industry in which they operate, as with any star player, most are driven by one underlying principle – sheer love of the game.

Speak with virtually any small business owner, be they restaurateur, CPA or developer (app, land or otherwise), and you'll hear similar themes echoed. Chief among them are passion, unswerving dedication and, above all else, a fundamental and seemingly overriding commitment to charting one's own course in life. It's a common thread that unites many entrepreneurs, no matter their level of success or chosen field, and one that binds almost all self-made professionals together. Some stories are inspirational, others heartbreaking, and still more so strange and unlikely you'd almost mistake them for fiction. Nonetheless, in years of founding, counseling and speaking professionally to small businesses and the fascinating individuals behind them, one thing yours truly has yet to encounter is a tale that's meaningless or uninspirational.

Something you can be certain of: Choosing to start a business, whether as a side project, part-time gig, or full-time enterprise, will irrevocably change your life. Irrespective of when the urge strikes, early or late in life, as a learning experience, it's also an endeavor that's destined to permanently ingrain itself upon your general outlook and view of the world. No matter if you're fresh out of school and itching to reinvent the high-tech universe, or an experienced professional committed to achieving success in a second career, be advised: Attempting to go it alone is destined to be a singular and unforgettable experience. Note that it's not uncommon to meet those who describe themselves as "serial" entrepreneurs who, after bootstrapping it once, have gone on to pursue numerous ventures in several unexpected and otherwise seemingly disparate fields.

Starting a business is many things… exciting, enriching, filled with anxiety and trepidation. But as a rule, one thing it's certainly not is for the faint of heart, or an experience you'll soon forget. The buck stops with entrepreneurs, meaning it's ultimately up to you to call the shots, make the hard decisions and always be your own champion in the face of harsh reality and overwhelming odds. Even when the chips are down though – and, as any veteran can tell you, you can expect to eat more ramen than caviar – you can take solace in having the guts to go for it. Few and far between are those who ever opt to cut ties with the world of salaried employment, and take control of their own fate. For a myriad of reasons both personal and financial, it bears remembering: Most never get the chance to be pioneers. Succeed or fail, it's a rare and beautiful thing to say you had the opportunity, let alone took the shot.

Happily, from housewives founding fashion empires in their back bedrooms to attorneys bidding the rat race adieu to open their own wine emporiums, more and more are choosing to spread their wings. No matter the impetus behind such initiatives, be grateful: All have, and continue to be, a tireless source of creativity and inspiration to us all. Nobody said their job was easy – despite the increasing array of tools and technology available to today's business owner, even local merchants are now being forced to compete 24/7, and on a global scale. But as you'll see reflected in examples throughout this book, growth opportunities are greater than ever for such enterprises thanks to an arsenal of high-tech advancements, including tablet PCs, smartphones, apps and social networks. Worth keeping in mind while you read, though: The more things change, the more certain fundamentals stay the same. Even in the 21st century, customer service remains paramount, and value still accrues most to entrepreneurs with the smarts and savvy to best leverage the tools at their disposal.

Certainly, the playing field is becoming increasingly level, with technology rapidly giving small business owners the means and power to compete with larger and better-funded concerns. But make no mistake: As ever, potential upsides are only what you make of them, and there remains no substitute for pure ingenuity and resourcefulness – the entrepreneur's most defining traits of all. Bearing this in mind, the hints, tips and strategies found throughout this book provide a sound starting point for discussion. Above all else though, it's our sincere hope that the following volume will inspire and spark the imagination. No matter how far it carries you, remember – no sound business plan remains static forever, or single overarching strategy applicable to all individuals and situations. Learning to plot one's own course and make the rules up as you go is the very essence of entrepreneurialism.

Technology's continued progress notwithstanding, the road ahead is neither easily charted nor certain. But armed with the information contained here, you'll be better equipped to meet the challenges its unforeseen twists and turns will inevitably present. To those dreaming of starting their own enterprise and lifelong entrepreneurs alike, we're proud to provide ongoing support and resources. Having personally founded enterprises small and large, and survived the vagaries of helming growing startups, we recognize the reality of the situation. For some "it's just business," but to you, it's so much more. We're grateful and honored for the chance to provide guideposts that can help ease your journey down the long, tumultuous and ultimately transcendental road that lies ahead.

Best practices and standards constantly change though, as do the means and channels through which working professionals and even entire industries operate. As you enjoy our books, videos and training products, or attend our keynote speeches and workshops, I'd like to personally invite you to join in the conversation via social media, and at our website. Wise business owners learn, grow and reinvent themselves daily: We wouldn't be here without your priceless insight, feedback and mentoring. Be sure to stop by and share your hard-won advice, or take a moment to say hello at the next industry event or tradeshow. It's always a pleasure to connect with fellow professionals – win or lose, even more so those who've had the guts and wherewithal to pursue their own personal vision.

If nothing else, we hope you take the following away from this manuscript: Triumph or falter, the only true failure lies in never having tried. Whether located in a plush high-rise or technically situated in the middle of a moldering basement, I look forward to seeing you in the boardroom…

Scott Steinberg
www.ASmallBusinessExpert.com

PART 1

MARKETING
BUILDING YOUR BRAND

Chapter 1
WHAT MAKES YOU SO SPECIAL?
BUILDING YOUR PERSONAL BRAND

Nobody likes a braggart. But everyone likes to feel that they stand for something. Small wonder then that in the 21st century, personal branding – the art of packaging and presenting yourself or your company like corporate giants such as Reebok and Pepsi would consumer products – has become so vital to both career and business development.

Credit tectonic shifts in both cultural norms and commercial realities: In a faster-paced, increasingly visual world where attention spans are shrinking, more parties are competing for less, let's be frank – out of sight is out of mind. Immediate and sustained visibility isn't just crucial to making sure you stand out from the endless barrage of white noise, let alone rivals competing for the same limited pool of dollars and resources. It also, for better or worse, increasingly defines public perception of who you are and what values you and your business represent.

Call it self-aggrandizing if you like. Label it indicative of a decline in social values if you wish. But make no bones about it: People tend to make snap judgments based on what they see at first glance (you know what they say about first impressions), and basic marketing principles still revolve around frequency and reach. Therefore, it's essential that if you want to be viewed a certain way, you must not only project the corresponding image at a glance, but also grab the reins and take control of your own fate, rather than letting others arbitrarily define you or your enterprise instead.

It's a point especially worth taking to heart in the age of online search engines, where research often amounts to typing a search query into a box and seeing what pops up. Quickly becoming key constituents' such as shoppers' and strategic partners' first port of call, the top three Google results – accurate or not – alone can oftentimes define your entire professional persona. Needless to say, it pays to be proactive about shaping public perception, as for many stakeholders that both individuals and enterprises will interface with, what they see is what they'll expect to get.

Thankfully, you don't need a celebrity stylist's eye for fashion or a Hollywood publicist's media savvy to give your personal or corporate image an extreme makeover. Looking to instantly boost your business, establish yourself as a subject matter expert or simply generate widespread awareness for your particular passion, field or cause? Here are five simple strategies that individuals and organizations alike can use to instantly set themselves apart from the pack.

1 Craft a Compelling Pitch – The first rule of personal branding: You need to be able to clearly define yourself, and sum up precisely what it is you and your company do, in 20-30 seconds or less. A concept known as the fabled "elevator pitch," it's a vital tool for defining public perception, and quickly summarizing personalities and organizations at a glance. When in doubt, make a simple matrix of the skills you feel you or your business excel at, and the personal qualities and values you're most proud of – then create a powerful and truthful description that best connects the dots. Ask yourself: How do I see myself? Are you a "web design guru," "leader in forensic accounting" or "online community manager?" Because that's how most others will categorize you mentally: As a short, descriptive tag that's lumped into a single grouping for convenient filing and reference.

To this extent, your pitch needs to be brief, to the point, and ensure that—as time-strapped individuals are wont to do—when you're quickly shunted into a specific subject grouping, it's the one that best matches your experience. That way, when the person in question has a need for a specific service, they know exactly whom to call. Note that the clearer and more succinct your talking points are, the better—delivery is most effective when shortened to one or two brief sentences. As a rule, to ensure maximum efficacy, messaging should be presented right up-front and consistent across all public-facing channels as well. Whether explaining yourself and what you do in person, or encapsulating your business' basic services in a press release, themes and mission statements should remain uniform and highly visible throughout.

Pro tip: Rather than vying for attention in an area that's saturated with rivals, strike where the competition isn't, and pick a niche that's clearly being underserved. That way, your voice won't just ring out louder—its echoes will also travel further. Wherever possible, try to pair descriptions with popular industry terms and search engine keywords as well. You may refer to yourself as an "IT expert," but if 99% of the world is searching for "network administrator," why not kill two birds with one stone? Free services like **Google Insights for Search** and **Google AdWords'** keyword tool can help you determine which phrases and terms are trending, and discover the most popular ways the world defines certain professions. As a bonus for those too preoccupied managing day-to-day operations to play "buzzword bingo," they may also provide added inspiration when looking for unique ways to define yourself.

2 Take Control of Your Image – Despite having said it once, we'll say it again, because it can't be stressed enough: Search engine marketing cannot be ignored. From prospective clients and business partners to job recruiters and HR experts, countless professionals (all increasingly strapped for time and bandwidth) are turning to services like **Google**, **Ask** and **Bing** to research specific topics, service providers and potential hires in ever-growing numbers. Therefore it's imperative that you tap into the power of these platforms to build brand awareness and reinforce the message you're trying to convey.

As a starter exercise, try inputting your name or your business's name in Google, and see what comes up. It's vital that the majority of results that appear – especially the first ones that pop up, as they're the likeliest to be clicked on – be those you want, and that all reinforce the same clear talking points. (As studies show, the first three search results command nearly 60% of the traffic, with performance falling sharply with each lower-ranked placement… Answers found on page two of Google search queries alone are 24 times less likely to be touched.) To this extent, as when registering a business website, you should not only own a website with your personal name as the domain (www.johnsmith.com) or a simple variation thereof (www. johnjaysmith.com). You should also have profiles on all major social networking services (Facebook, Twitter, LinkedIn, Plaxo, etc.) under the same name, or specific keywords ("IPAttorney," "FreelanceWriter," "HomeAVExpert," etc.) that reinforce what your personal brand stands for.

Also keep in mind – virtually everything you say or do online is publicly visible and can linger in perpetuity on the Internet. So always think twice before you post something dubious or upload pictures from last night's party to your Facebook or Google+ profile, regardless of whether you've preconfigured privacy settings or setup limited social circles. If it's not something you'd feel comfortable sharing in front of coworkers or clients at the office, it's not something you should be projecting into cyberspace. Note that anything can be perceived as amateurish, distasteful or damning when taken out of context, especially in an age where tweets and status updates are being used as evidence or part of courtroom testimony. Before jokingly criticizing a competitor or gently ribbing a coworker, it bears remembering: Professionalism pays. Like poor career decisions or unprofessional partings with prior employers, you never know when your actions may return to haunt you.

3 Make Your Point Heard – Many hesitate to speak up, for fear of criticism or ridicule. But that's exactly the dilemma in an era where so many are competing for so little – it's the squeaky wheels that get the grease. Keep in mind: At its heart, personal branding is about establishing yourself or your business as a subject matter expert who brings unique, indispensable services to the table, not just another faceless cog in the wheel. To this effect, you need to create platforms (**websites**, **blogs**, **podcasts**, **self-published books/magazines**, **online video channels**, etc.) that can help broadcast your views to as many members of a specific audience as possible and galvanize support and community input around them. All of these vehicles should also be stamped with your signature name, logo, imagery and overall sensibilities.

Once you build these platforms, it pays to pump out content through them that illustrates your expertise as studiously as possible, whether via articles, surveys, opinions, research reports or topical analysis. Countless platforms exist to help spread the word and grow your readership or viewing audience as well, from Facebook and Twitter accounts to LinkedIn groups and **custom-built communities** or social networks. Alternately, you can always blog for popular media outlets, submit bylined articles to trade magazines in exchange for a picture and bio, or participate as a speaker at trade events. Along the same lines, don't hesitate to share content with or send updates to fellow subject matter experts either, as they can help to cross-promote and generate awareness for your initiatives. Essentially, you don't just want to be active and highly visible – you want to be a strong, stable and welcome presence everywhere your audience goes.

Simply put, you can't afford to be shy. From cluttered inboxes to constantly jangling cell phones and a non-stop barrage of coworker and client queries, today's workplace is filled with ambient noise and distraction. You've got to speak up – and, most importantly, have something strong and meaningful to say – if you want to be heard.

4 Be Generous with Your Time – Doing other professionals and business owners favors, taking the time to answer reader questions or making a point to contribute to charitable causes that benefit your field as a whole may not seem cost-effective from a pure monetary standpoint. But acts of kindness and generosity aren't just good for building character. They also serve to generate goodwill and help build invaluable relationships and contacts that can pay off immeasurably in the long run.

Not only do all present great opportunities to establish trust, grow your personal or professional network and make a positive impact – you never know when they'll lead to a new strategic connection, unexpected client referral or lucrative job opportunity. And there's no quicker way to build support for a cause or make an unexpected ally than by spending time and effort to go above and beyond the call of duty. It doesn't just speak to personal values and work ethic. It also presents the perfect chance to demonstrate your knowledge and expertise.

Whether you believe in karma or not, it's essential to "pay it forward," as the saying goes. A moment's kindness can often echo for years, and competitive as the modern commercial environment has become, you can never have too many friends out there. True masters of personal branding understand it's not about the marketing. It's a vehicle through which you can open doors, build bridges and create opportunity for yourself and those who surround you. It never hurts to provide those in need a favor – and, in fact, it may help build a network of peers whose generosity and insight you can call on for invaluable advice or support in a pinch. Always be open and generous with your support, as you never know… in business, the smallest decision may come back to reward or haunt you someday.

5 Get Out and Mingle – Whether using blog posts, tweets, press releases, online newswires, your professional Facebook fan page or free services that connect experts with enthusiasts or reporters to build public and media rapport, accessibility is the name of the game. Not only do people need to know you're out there – they also need to know where and how to reach you, that you're available to connect as needed, and that you will respond to requests for outreach in a timely fashion. This doesn't mean having to broadcast your personal information to the world or staying up until 3 a.m. responding to 400 emails every night. But it does necessitate that you not build too many layers of insulation between yourself and incoming queries, and be respectful of acknowledging people's questions and feedback (even if it's just through a series of blog posts).

The bottom line: If you want to be a go-to guy or gal, you've got to earn people's trust. That means not only being genuine, as good as your word and capable of delivering high-quality work or insights on tight turnaround. It also means being willing to signal via your actions that you don't just hear what they're saying, but that you are further actively seeking out others' opinions and assigning weight and import to both sides of the conversation.

Make Yourself More Marketable

Wise professionals know that personal branding isn't just for entrepreneurs, as even salaried workers are self-employed to some extent (their biggest client just happens to be their current employer). So for potential job seekers hunting for positions in today's constantly-shifting marketplace, with more competing for fewer positions, consider putting yourself in harried employers' shoes and asking: What makes me stand out from the crowd? Granted, chest-thumping egotism remains distasteful as ever. But how you package and present yourself also speaks volumes. Here's how, with little cost and effort, you can multiply personal equity tenfold.

Do the Math – Education is expensive, but ignorance remains costlier still: Keeping one's skill set current is vital. While others waste time atrophying to daytime talk shows, realize – now's the time to double down and invest in yourself. Can't afford to go back to school? Try an online degree, or sharpen your skills with free Internet webinars, interactive tutorials and downloadable reference volumes, or tap into complementary seminars and classes, such as those offered by **iTunes U**. The world constantly evolves, and to keep pace, you must as well. Failing to remain competitive can actually cost more in the long run.

Speak Up – Don't hesitate – create. Use blogs, bylined articles, podcasts, self-published manuscripts, webcam videos, research projects, surveys and social networks to spread your message. What we do in the off-hours speaks equal volumes, if not more, than those formally spent on the clock. Thankfully, with cyberspace's countless cost-effective tools at your fingertips, it's easy to become a recognized thought leader and make your voice heard. Value accrues to those who can show employers that they're passionate subject matter experts and can make things happen with or without a major multinational corporation backing them.

Meet and Greet – These words will change your life: "You are who you know." Via services like LinkedIn, Plaxo and Facebook, it's easy to connect with peers and potential mentors worldwide. Like becoming active in online forums, trade associations and professional organizations, attending virtual tradeshows can also provide career-making contacts as well. Given that over 80% of actual job openings go unpublished in the current commercial era, it literally pays to mingle. Through clever networking and positioning, some savvy individuals have even managed to talk prospective employers into creating an entirely new position just for them.

Spread the Word – With so much noise out there, it's imperative that you stay top of mind. Website posts, newsletters, Twitter updates, press releases, stories freely swapped with trade journals in exchange for a published link or personal bio – all make effective self-promotions. While there's a fine line between annoyance and assertiveness, one can't afford to be coy. Remember: The greater your visibility, the likelier you'll be clients' first port of call. Don't be discouraged if you don't get traction immediately either – trust isn't built overnight, and familiarity breeds awareness and comfort.

Online Job Hunting Tips

GET HIRED WITH THESE SIMPLE TRICKS

Use Keywords – With most resume review processes now automated, it's vital that you employ simple, search-friendly terms (e.g., "customer service representative," "executive assistant" or "marketing director") throughout. Less than 10% of resumes are ever actually viewed by a real person. Hint: Keywords can typically be filched right from the job description itself.

Customize Submissions – One size does not fit all. Every cover letter and resume should be tailored to fit the potential employer and position, mixing and matching the traits and skills that clearly communicate why you're the best man/woman for the job. Always follow up on resume and cover letter submission within two weeks as well.

Focus Your Efforts – Professional recruiters and sites like Monster, TheLadders, Yahoo! Careers or CareerBuilder.com can help, but you'll often get further picking 5-10 dream companies to concentrate on (under 5% get jobs through these large sites). You're also likelier to have better success with highly-targeted solutions such as local and specialist sites (AtlantaJobs, TVJobs, TechCareers, etc.). Don't just sign up for emails on job updates either; research these firms online and find ways – personal blogs, official newsgroups, etc. – to directly connect with employers and let them know you're interested/available.

Stay Visible – Use social networks (LinkedIn, Plaxo, Facebook, Twitter, BizNik, etc.) to source endorsements from colleagues, conduct business outreach, establish your expert credentials and let others know you're seeking employment. Participate in professional online forums, blogs and chat rooms wherever possible to build credibility and rapport too. Informational interviews – asking someone in a desired position to describe the day-to-day ins/outs of their job – can also be hugely effective, and (most importantly) make you hard to forget. As many as four in five jobs go unlisted, so direct networking can be your best bet for landing that dream position.

Chapter 2
SELF PUBLISHING SOLUTIONS:
HOW TO START A BUSINESS OVERNIGHT

From starting one's own fashion label to becoming a high-flying media mogul or publishing the next great novel, everyone's got their own vision of the American Dream. Thankfully today, courtesy of countless online self-publishing services, making it a reality is oftentimes as easy as simply clicking on a website.

Credit a wealth of cost-effective options that let you print on-demand, sell everything from candy to t-shirts directly to shoppers and instantly get your products in front of a massive global audience. Suddenly, literally anyone can take advantage of custom design, outsourced order fulfillment, automated payment processing and worldwide shipping solutions to start their own record label or launch tomorrow's most addictive software app.

Even better still – most options are generally affordable enough (ranging anywhere from $10-$1000 dollars and up), that you don't have to sell a kidney or beg friends and family for cash to fund the enterprise. And even if you did, crowdsourced funding solutions such as the following services can help you raise seed money well in advance of even building a formal prototype:

- **Kickstarter**
- **IndieGogo**
- **Ulule**
- **RocketHub**
- **33Needs**
- **Spot.us**

Crowdfunding offers a new way to raise money for any startup.

Looking to start a lucrative side project, build the startup of your dreams or create the ultimate social networking app? Stop idling and making excuses, because there's never been a better, or more affordable, time to launch your enterprise. From books to bedroom accessories, gourmet edibles to must-have software programs, the following solutions can instantly put you in business overnight:

Artwork, Clothing, and Collectibles

The globe's largest online art fair, **Etsy** makes it possible to send handcrafted goods including pottery, furniture, jewelry, knitting and purses to millions of fans of fine Bohemian wares. Set up stall there, and you can sell virtually any crazy item that you can dream up, from Twilight-themed pet collars to necklaces adorned with George Clooney's likeness.

Fancy yourself a fashion plate instead? Try **CafePress**, where you can build your own online clothing boutique and stock it with custom baseball caps, hoodies, boxers and baby clothes. (Hint: Any gags involving bacon are already way overdone.) **Spreadshirt** also lets you upload t-shirt designs and build personalized aprons, messenger bags and other goodies, while **PrintMojo** provides the tools you need to make and sell your own wearable slogans.

Should your tastes range more towards stickers and kitschy souvenirs, **Zazzle** makes a solid pit stop too. Hit the site up to design individualized mugs, magnets, greeting cards, mouse pads, binders and beer steins. Musicians especially will dig its ability to keep you well-stocked in custom merchandise (although, as with anything printed in short runs, base prices won't exactly be rock-bottom). **PrintableMemories** further makes it possible to put one's own stamp on pillows, photo tins, jewelry bottles and other assorted objects.

Aspiring photographers might also turn to **Snapfish**, **Shutterfly** and **Picaboo** to produce coffee table-ready collections of their work. Images – whether original or affordably licensed from stock image collections such as **Shutterstock** and **iStockPhoto** – can further be appended onto stationary, address labels, coffee mugs, serving trays or anything else that can benefit from a candid close-up of your pet Pomeranian.

Books and Magazines

Why kill trees? In many cases, a nicely-illustrated PDF digital document makes a perfectly good, and readily distributable, way to spread your book, paper, research report, journal or publication across the Internet. (Or, for that matter, syndicate to desktop and laptop PCs, plus compatible smartphones, eReaders and tablet devices.) Several online converters (just Google "convert Word to PDF") let you transform Microsoft Word documents into PDF files, including **Adobe's own official service**. Microsoft Office 2007 (and later edition) users can even download **free plug-ins** that let you save right out to the format, creating digital manuscripts suitable for viewing on the iPad, Kindle, Nook and more.

Custom email newsletters may further provide a solid alternative to traditional print runs, and offer detailed analytics that let you keep track of how often they're opened and who's reading what. Among other popular services, **MailChimp**, **Campaign Monitor**, **Constant Contact**, **Benchmark Email** and **MadMimi** stand out.

Eat your heart out, Condé Nast, as well… Blogging platforms ranging from **WordPress** to **TypePad**, **Blogger** and **Movable Type** also allow anyone to become a magazine publishing magnate overnight – even faster if they buy readymade plug-and-play **templates** ($20-$50 on average) providing preconfigured features and graphics. (Shh, don't tell: Many of today's top newsstand publishers and cable networks even use these software solutions to power their own sites, backed by "plug-ins," or downloadable add-ons, that introduce endless features and functionality.)

Need a fancier or more customized option? While pre-made visual templates provide an attractive and professional-looking paint job for mere tens of dollars, a personally tailored look and layout can easily run you $1,000-$8,000. Still, it's a small price to pay compared with setting up newsstand distribution, which you can either secure or circumvent using small-run print and/or online manuscripts provided by the likes of **Zinio**, **MagCloud** and **Issuu**.

Enamored with bound and printed volumes? **Lulu.com** can be a handy way to produce paperbacks or hardbacks, as well as yearbooks, cookbooks, CDs, DVDs, calendars and other keepsakes that look as good as professionally-produced counterparts. Granted, if you're not technically inclined, some outside graphic and visual layout assistance may be needed. (Note that while we've used the service successfully in conjunction with artwork and spreads commissioned from professional graphic designers, others who've used their custom in-house editorial or aesthetic services complain of mixed results.) You can also use the platform to secure an ISBN and distribution into vendors like Amazon.com, Barnes and Noble, iBooks (for use on iPhone and iPad) and the Nook bookstore.

Similar caveats apply to **iUniverse** (full disclosure: we've also printed with this service with mixed returns), and a multitude of other vendors including **Blurb**, **Wordclay**, **Xlibris**, **CreateSpace** and **AuthorHouse**. Oh, and lest ye receive a nasty surprise, realize: As with any on-demand item, you'll pay through the nose, even for your own books, in limited print runs, with volume discounts awarded based on larger orders. Then again, you could always go the Kindle route: Books for Amazon's suite of eReaders, including the Kindle Fire, can be pushed in minutes via the **Kindle Direct Publishing** service.

Food and Drink

Mom and Pop stores or independent food and beverage providers have a couple of good options for getting their five-star chili or secret cookie mix into the hands of the general public. A culinary equivalent to Etsy, **Foodzie** lets you sell everything from candy to coffee and meat directly to hungry shoppers via custom tasting boxes. **Foodoro** (which claims a more highbrow stance) also makes a welcome platform for serving up vegan, organic and confectionary treats. As for actually whipping the stuff up, well – sadly, you'll still need a spare kitchen and lots of baking sheets. Note that if you do have a food product you're looking to promote, you might consider making outreach to food blogs and foodie social networking sites like **iMunchie.com**, **Gojee** and **FoodCandy**.

Music and Video

Creating your own **podcast**, or digital audio recording ready for Internet distribution, is easy enough to accomplish with a $10 headset and free recording software such as **Audacity**. (Note that other tools like **REAPER**, **ProTools** and **GarageBand** can also help rock star hopefuls.) Once built, talk programming or musical performances can then be syndicated onto Apple's iTunes or through your own site to help find an audience. Afterwards, TuneCore and CDBaby can help you get tracks out over the airwaves via eMusic, Amazon MP3, Rhapsody and other services. CDBaby even has a partnership with Rumblefish that lets independent artists license music for use in marketing campaigns, social media efforts, YouTube/online videos, video games and more.

Becoming the next Steven Spielberg is also fairly straightforward (well, talent and vision aside), courtesy of a range of new budget high-definition video cameras. Models like the Bloggie 3D and Kodak PlayFull (all under $250, with average pocket units going for less than $100) can help. We personally recommend the old tried-and-true Kodak Zi8, which offers external microphone support, allowing for superior audio. A webcam ($20-$50) such as those offered by Logitech or camera-equipped mobile device such as the iPad 2 and iPhone 4S can also provide a ready way to record the next viral video sensation. Mind you, footage won't be as stunning or crisp as if produced with a proper crew and high-end equipment. But for basic online distribution, such options generally do the job quite nicely.

Once clips are recorded and edited, just upload to YouTube, Vimeo, Viddler, Metacafe or other online aggregators for sharing and embedding, or you can simply distribute them on your own site. Live streaming services such as Justin.tv, BlogTV, uStream.tv and Stickam also let you become a talk show host in no time flat, though they aren't for wilting daises. With Android and Apple iOS apps like SocialCam and Qik readily available, what are you waiting for? Your 15 seconds of fame awaits…

Software and Video Games

While there's no simple way to create software for PCs, smartphones and video game systems (alas, they haven't found a way to automate programmers, artists, producers and quality assurance testing departments yet), you don't have to be a computer science major to self-publish.

To create programs for Android devices or the iPhone (the latter of which costs $99 for the developer's toolkit), you can seek help from outside contractors at sites like oDesk or Guru. com. Other options like iPhoneAppQuotes and Get Apps Done also promise to put you in touch with capable coders and artists. Be forewarned, however: Any outsourced project requires stringent management and oversight, and none of these sites guarantee quality of output or any return on investment.

Entrepreneurs hoping to make their mark on the gaming scene can further try Microsoft's App Hub, which lets you design for Xbox 360 and Windows Phone. Software suites like Torque Game Engine, The 3D Gamemaker and Adventure Game Studio also offer an outlet for custom productions, as does PlayFirst's free Playground SDK. But once again, if you're not blessed with software coding or 3D animation skills, you'll need help from external sources.

Social Networks

Facebook and Twitter are nice, but what if you want to establish yourself as a subject matter expert on a niche topic, or connect with like-minded colleagues, customers and peers in a single, specific industry? Services like **Ning**, **CrowdVine** and **GoingOn** all offer readymade platforms for building your own community, as do alternate options including **Wall. fm**, **SocialEngine**, and **Mixxt**. Used wisely, such vehicles could allow you to create a captive audience whose screen you're in front of several times daily – and one ever-ready to purchase your latest books, DVDs or research reports.

Conclusion

Contrary to popular folklore, you don't have to be exceptionally rich, smart or well-connected to bring a company to life these days. All it takes is a little time and dedication. (OK, possibly a talented designer, videographer, programmer, seamstress, and/or chef, depending on your chosen field…) But realistically, hairpiece aside, there's nothing stopping you from becoming the next Donald Trump. With the Web at your fingertips, you're literally just seconds away from becoming a self-made entrepreneur.

Become an Online Video Sensation

Buoyed by heightened broadband penetration and viewers' insatiable appetite for original content, demand for video is skyrocketing, as consumers continue to gravitate en masse from television towards online aggregators like **Vimeo**, **Viddler** and **Crackle**. (Not to mention premium content providers like **Hulu** and **Revision3**.) That includes category leader **YouTube**, which now serves over 4 billion views a day and 21.9 billion views a month according to comScore, though even that figure pales before the 42.6 billion videos that U.S. households watch in the same 30-day period. (Amazingly, an hour of video is now uploaded every second.) Likewise, with 184 million Internet users enjoying online video content for an average of 21.1 hours each in October 2011 alone, it's obvious that corresponding marketing opportunities are also growing by leaps and bounds. Knowing this, if online video isn't a current cornerstone of your current promotional or public relations strategy, it's obvious that it should be.

As an added bonus, virtual distribution channels are a dime a dozen nowadays, and all the more accessible and attractive given their ability to host and serve video at no cost to you, the creator. Just be careful to read the fine print: Some may attempt to automatically assume ownership or distribution rights of all footage uploaded to their service, while others might place frustrating caps on video size and length. Still, offering the ability to easily "embed" video links into websites, thereby letting you seamlessly integrate recorded spots into existing corporate web pages, blogs and social networks, there's no beating their value, ease of use, or proven ability to reach end-users.

Once upon a time, video production was the sole province of businesses with thousands of dollars to burn. Nowadays, it's accessible to enterprises of any scope – even lone individuals working out of a spare bedroom or garage. Thankfully, creating effective online viral campaigns doesn't have to cost a small fortune or even require hiring a dedicated camera crew. Ready to hit play on your own custom broadcast initiative? Following is everything you need to know to design and build an online effective video-based campaign (note: acting lessons sold separately).

Choose the Right Hardware – While you'll still get the best results from a proper video camera (see: models by Samsung, Canon, Panasonic, etc.), pocket camcorders such as the Kodak PlaySport and Zoom Q3HD can all produce perfectly Web-worthy results too. Sony's Bloggie 3D even lets you shoot in full 3D for under $200, while the iPhone 4 offers 1080p HD filming right from your pocket. Whichever route you choose, pick a model that shoots in 720p high-definition (HD) minimum, and offers an external microphone input. Ideally, you'll want a unit that supports expandable SD memory cards or external archival solutions as well, allowing you to store more hours of footage in any sitting. It's also important to go hands-on with all options before buying to gauge the capability of extras such as low-light filming performance, image stabilization, color, clarity and battery life. If you're not technically inclined, you'll additionally want to look at a device that offers ready one-touch uploads to photo and video aggregation services like Flickr and YouTube.

Pick Your Battles – You can't please everyone or create much noise attempting to scream into a wind tunnel. So before filming the first frame, make certain you've got a clear idea of the topic you'd like to cover, and determine the conceptual angle you'll take to differentiate your viewpoint from the thousands already cluttering up cyberspace. (As a simple litmus test, just ask yourself: "If I'm an everyday viewer browsing for information on the Internet or social networking services, what's to make my idea stand out from countless others?") Also consider what form the video should take: news byte, expert interview, testimonials reel, making-of clip, behind-the-scenes documentary, comedic skit, etc. The options here are infinite, offering little excuse to skimp on originality. To succeed with video programming (or any online content), remember: You need to take a singular, unique approach that instantly makes your program pop off the screen and be memorable to viewers as a result.

Take a Stance – Video's greatest strength is arguably the sense of empathy and familiarity it creates between viewers and on-screen talent. So don't be coy – get out there and make your opinion heard. This doesn't mean you have to be rude, obnoxious or controversial: Just engaging enough to catch someone's eye, and convey your own unique sense of personality.

It isn't just about connecting with an audience or more effectively getting a point across. It also comes down to establishing a unique point of view and sense of perspective that others can discuss, debate and/or galvanize behind. If all you're saying is what's on the teleprompter, or something audiences can get from dozens of other individuals or media outlets, what's to make you intriguing or noteworthy? Positive, negative, completely off the wall… pick an approach and run with it. After all, why should anyone bother tuning in and listening if you're not speaking up and saying something of interest?

Grab Viewers' Attention – Between constant interruptions from social networks, buzzing Blackberries and everyday work and life, audiences' spare time is shorter and attention span more divided than ever. So if you can't excite or engage them in the first 5-15 seconds, it's time to rethink your approach. The opening moments of any video should be brisk, arresting and straight to the point, delivering the program's unique topic and stance up front, as well as a taste of what's to come. To this extent, exciting teaser shots, tempting hooks and energetic personalities can all work wonders, as can the promise of must-see testimonials, lessons and viewpoints. Translation: Go big or go home right off the bat, and don't slack off on the back-end either, as failure to maintain a sense of pacing or excitement quickly leads to viewer fatigue and attrition. If this means making clips shorter (we've found 90 seconds to 3 minutes max to be an ideal length for short-form Web content), so be it. The key is always to say more with less, be it pictures, animations, diagrams, witty one-liners or cutting insights.

Don't Overdo It – You don't need glossy production values, high-concept sets or fancy editing tricks to engage audiences on the Web, where a rawer, more organic form of dialogue is encouraged. That doesn't mean you should skimp on quality – nothing shatters suspension of disbelief or takes a viewer out of the experience quicker than poor audio, worse lighting or endless technical hiccups. Rather, scenarios and subjects should seem compelling and delivered in a plausible context. Likewise, dialogue should feel normal and off-the-cuff – the same way it would when talking to friends, colleagues or associates in real life. Not only are today's audiences smarter, better informed and more empowered than ever, they're also more likely not to identify with quips that come off as too canned, or spray-tanned hosts that hope to substitute slick talk for substance. Ultimately, whether selling shoes or revealing the secrets of search engine optimization, you're trying to package and present a compelling tale that speaks to others in a language they can understand. And – especially for more informal items like brief hands-on product demos, event-based coverage, video blogs and office tours – that doesn't mean having to dress everything up with fancy scripts, snazzy animations or mind-blowing 3D special effects.

Keep the Message Simple – Too many video campaigns, even multimillion-dollar Super Bowl ads, forget the cardinal rule: Keep it simple, stupid. It pays to establish very quickly off the bat what the core point(s) are that you're trying to make. Subsequent imagery and commentary, though informative and entertaining where appropriate, should simply serve to reinforce these highlights. An easy way to stay on track: Pick one to three key bullet points you'd like to get across before beginning, and use them as a guidepost throughout production. Just be careful not to err too much on the side of repetition, which gets monotonous, or lean too heavily on surprise, humor or excitement at the expense of clarity. If viewers can't comprehend or remember the point you're trying to make, regardless of whether the clip is low- or high-concept, it's still a wasted effort.

Focus on Value Creation – Ask yourself: What's your time worth? Because that's the same question viewers will be pondering, whether knowingly or not, every time they decide to tune into a video program, or skip it in favor of getting work done or idling with other pursuits instead. As such, it's essential that if you're going to ask someone for a chunk of their day or, tougher still, to actively take action and reach into their wallet, you offer something of meaningful value as part of the trade-off. Simple ways to do so include, but aren't limited to, offering educational content (i.e. through an expert how-to), exclusive access (e.g. a one-on-one Q&A with a sought-after speaker) or a unique perspective (example: a noteworthy pundit's view of why the latest business trend is secretly a non-starter). Consider what has real, tangible value to your viewer, and provide it – only then have you earned the right to ask for something in return.

Don't Be Afraid to Laugh – Transparency can be a tricky subject for many businesses keen to sell a particular product or service. Push a topic too overtly, and viewers tune it out. Take too soft an approach and you risk them not making the connection or identifying with your brand. Sometimes, bridging the gap can be as easy as saying "we're here for a reason, you're here for a reason, so let's not be shy about it." To this extent, breaking the fourth wall and either speaking directly to the viewer or letting them know you're aware of the irony of the situation can help bridge the gap. Just be careful to use the technique sparingly, as it won't fit all scenarios, and don't lean too self-ironic, or you risk damaging the credibility of yourself and your wares.

Include a Call to Action – Any video can act as a simple branding exercise, serving to raise the profile of you or your business. But those intended to generate a measurable audience reaction need to ask viewers to take an actionable step in order to generate one. This call to action can take the form of a simple web link ("Visit now to cast your vote!"), request for viewer feedback ("Email us your questions for answering in our next episode"), dial-in number ("Call now – the first 100 viewers will receive a special bonus gift") or any number of alternatives. For example, one of the most interesting viral programs in recent memory involved players choosing which character would be a video game's official spokesman by "voting" with their clicks every time they chose to view a clip or passed links to do so along to friends. The lesson here: Creativity pays, but interactivity is more important still – if you want to derive real value from your videos, repeat as follows: Passivity is a thing of the past.

Spread the Word – Videos can certainly snowball and become huge hits through word-of-mouth channels. But to get to that point, they first need to reach critical mass. You can improve chances of clips generating huge public awareness by placing them on many popular portals such as **YouTube**, **Metacafe**, **Vimeo** and **Viddler**. Even more important, though: Make sure you get the word out about them to aid in viewer discovery. All clips you create should be not only readily embeddable on blogs and web pages, but also fully supported via press releases, social media mentions and other public relations tools that help spread the word. Oh, and don't be offended if you don't score the next viral video hit on your first try – competition is massive. Inside tip: It always helps if you keep videos "evergreen" by not tying them to specific dates, products or topical events. That way, they never seem dated and are ready to re-promote the second data theft, Internet privacy or other featured topics become en vogue again.

Examples to help you get started can be found below.

Click Below to See Our Shows:

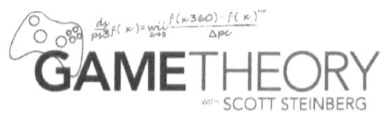

Chapter 3
MAKE YOUR BRAND POP: TODAY'S HOTTEST HIGH-TECH MARKETING TRENDS

So you've started to build your brand – congratulations! The next step is making it stand out among the hundreds of other products or services that will be your direct competitors. Don't have much of a marketing budget or expertise in the advertising field? Never fear – in this chapter, we'll show you how businesses of any size and experience level can make their voice heard, and without having to bet the proverbial farm to do so.

Naturally, every entrepreneur worth their weight in VC or angel investment hopes to discover new ways to grow revenues, increase sales and boost customer satisfaction. The fundamental problem: How do you compete against the Best Buys, Targets and Sears of the world for shoppers' attention, let alone disposable dollars, when your advertising budget barely buys enough share of voice to choke out a feeble whimper by comparison? Luckily, online technology and social media services prove the great evener.

An affordable alternative to expensive print, online and TV buys, high-tech marketing solutions level the playing field by letting you craft clever campaigns, easily connect with customers and cost-effectively provide arresting deals, discounts and promotions. In fact, thanks to the magic of the web and social media, from unique value-adds to creative contests, giveaways and online bargains, a variety of novel campaigns can quickly be assembled to match any budget. Here are eight cutting-edge marketing strategies that can help you quickly dial up results without dipping too heavily into your reserves.

1 **Social Media Programs** – Paid media can be effective, but it's also expensive. Merchants targeting local audiences on shoestring budgets can use social media platforms like Facebook, Twitter, Pinterest, Instagram and Google Plus to attract customers instead. But offering eye-opening incentives including steep discounts, free samples or unique hands-on trials is imperative to prompting viral pass-along. Programs such as two-for-one deals, bonus gifts with purchase and exclusive events ("Seasonal wine tasting and fashion show tonight – get a sneak peek at our new collection!") can all drive foot traffic, siphon customers from competitors and aid with lead generation. To ensure beleaguered shoppers don't discount them, though, you'll need to employ singularly original or arresting bargains. Splurging on customers using loss leaders (e.g., gift-wrapped dog treats with every grooming) and splashy time-limited promotions ("Live concert featuring the hottest local bands free today only!") not only helps generate direct prospects. It also allows you to create sampling opportunities, promote to a captive audience and, while consumers are actively engaged, potentially drive interest in higher-margin goods.

2 **Affiliate and Referral Marketing Programs** – Given word-of-mouth's growing influence on today's household purchasing decisions, it literally pays to turn fans of your business into evangelists. The best way to recruit them: Incentivize conversation by providing eye-catching offers and savings, and compensate those that generate direct leads with exclusive discounts, gifts and cash rewards. Using software tools such as those offered by providers like Extole, DirectTrack and ReferralCandy, you can create customized referral programs for almost any industry. ("Refer a pal, get $20! Click here to send Facebook friends a code for 60% off!") Distributable via social networks, widgets, apps and email, white-label solutions not only offer wide flexibility across devices, platforms and promotions, but they also make it easy to track ads from click to purchase and conscript an army of credible sales associates working on a strictly commission basis.

3 **Custom Content and Publications** – Resourceful entrepreneurs can also give shoppers the gift of more precious moments to spend with friends and family by providing time-saving hints and advice. Email marketing services ConstantContact, iContact and MadMimi let you send digital newsletters straight to shoppers' inboxes for a fraction of the cost of print mailers, and enable content sharing through social networks. Popular service MailChimp even allows gorgeous, customized mailings to be sent free in small quantities, while upgrades allow you to track viewers' social media profiles and send targeted emails via Facebook, Twitter, Flickr or LinkedIn. Couple with links to bargains, storefronts and online videos (effortless to upload and host on providers like YouTube, Vimeo and Metacafe, then embed on your own site) to enhance SEO and user engagement. Beyond highlighting your expertise, all can enhance your reach, keep bargains top of mind and help alleviate shoppers' stress while building brand awareness.

4 **Mobile and Location-Based Marketing** – Over 420 million smartphones were sold in 2011 alone according to IMS Research, many containing built-in GPS devices that actively monitor users' locations. Letting you speak to customers at the right time and place when they're in a shopping mood, mobile and location-based marketing services like Geotoko, Placecast and Xtify can potentially help close more deals. Providing users with discounts, giveaways and specials via text message, pop-up alert or email, you can also integrate marketing with services like Foursquare and Yelp to tie campaigns to specific stores or locations. Additionally, mobile commerce app Zaarly recently introduced free alerts to let businesses know when local residents have posted a request that they can fulfill. Top local search engine Milo (available online or as a smartphone app) even lets you update inventory and prices in real-time, allowing small- and medium-sized business owners to advertise bargains and put their catalogue in front of millions of neighborhood shoppers. From unique apps that send notifications even when they're closed to search engines that serve up special offers based on zip code, choices continue to grow. Letting you reach customers right when they're weighing their options, location-based services can help you steal a sale right out from under a competitor's feet.

5 **QR Codes** – Another handy feature many smartphones and tablets with built-in cameras such as the iPhone and iPad enjoy: the ability to scan Quick Response (QR) codes, which you can readily get from providers like **Qurify**, **Kaywa** and **Delivr**. These high-tech symbols, which operate similarly to retail barcodes, can beam over instant savings or provide access to useful online information. Add them to signs, print ads, business cards and brochures, and customers can quickly access coupons, download menus on-demand or even see how low your prices compare to rivals'. Simple bonuses they offer might include providing free holiday recipes to go with every dining set, complimentary music downloads with a new stereo or videos showing products you're selling in action. Letting you offer everything from suggestions on matching accessories to go with that blouse to downloadable driving directions, potential applications are endless. Just be sure each offers customers meaningful rewards and ties a call-to-action to programs ("Take our survey to win a dream voyage to Europe!") to maximize performance.

QR codes can work hard for your business and there are several free services that let you easily create them and track results.

6 **Discounts and Deals** – With value still paramount for millions of households and competition for shoppers' shrinking attention spans fiercer than ever, many entrepreneurs are increasingly coupling door-busting offers with regular distribution through daily deal services. Providers like **Groupon**, **Living Social**, **Amazon Local** and **Google Offers** can potentially put savings in front of millions for a slice of each purchase. Letting customers register to receive arresting bargains on spas, restaurants, movie theaters and more via email, all offer opportunities to help marketing programs connect with households trying to stretch every dollar. You can even set minimum purchase quantities required before discounts activate. Likewise, savvy marketers are also leveraging bargain-hunting services like **FatWallet**, **RetailMeNot** and **DealsPl.us** to reach today's most price-sensitive buyers. Issuing discount coupon codes, printable vouchers and unique presents for gift shoppers themselves ("Free leather carrying case with purchase") can help entice cost-conscious customers back into the fold. As an added bonus, for everyday users who stumble across them, they also create excitement and word-of-mouth buzz around seemingly elite offers that needn't dent your bottom line due to limited redemption periods or production runs.

7 **Contests and Giveaways** – The virtual equivalent of dropping a business card in a fishbowl for a free lunch, enticing customers to sign-up for generic online newsletters and email blasts is often just as difficult. To boost conversation rates and motivate audiences, instead offer value-adding content ("One-of-a-kind recipes delivered right to your inbox!"), interactive promotions that put applicants front and center, and more stirring rewards. Wherever possible, invite users to participate by submitting videos, photos, stories and other personal touches ("Tell us your worst birthday gift!"). Likewise, convert winning submissions into community spotlights, whether by highlighting contributors online, incorporating their submissions into ad campaigns, or making victors featured guests of honor at neighborhood events. Giveaway prizes should also reinforce the promotion's theme, provide unique experiences or play to wish-fulfillment. **Hint:** "Cozy up with a romantic five-course Italian meal with seasonal wine pairing" sounds better than "dinner for two at Alfredo's."

8 **Keywords and Online Advertising** – According to the Ponemon Institute, a full third of holiday shoppers were expected to spend more money online than in-store in 2011, and 37% and 12%, respectively, to make gift-giving purchases via smartphone or tablet. Knowing this, no matter your desired budget or audience, purchasing targeted keywords on popular search engines like **Bing** and **Google** can put you in front of prospective buyers right where they're doing their primary research. Coupled with custom geographic/demographic targeting and personalized scheduling and spending levels, choosing specific keywords and terms can prove a highly effective sales tactic. For maximum impact, use more detailed search terms (e.g., "custom cars New York" vs. "car kits") and less popular phrases. (Placements are sold via silent auction, meaning purchasing lightly-contested terms may offer a better share of voice at lower cost, and more click-throughs.) Inside tip: If you're feeling more naughty than nice, you can also buy up keywords related to competing products.

Chapter 4
TOP ONLINE MARKETING STRATEGIES

Business owners looking to grow their online audience have more options for building website traffic than ever. Some buy paid search engine placements via Google AdWords or Microsoft Advertising's adCenter for Bing or Yahoo. Others take out classifieds or sponsorships on sites like CraigsList and Yelp. Still more target placements by age, region and consumer interest courtesy of online ad networks, Facebook, in-app advertising solutions, mobile location-based services (e.g. Yowza!!) or daily deal networks such as Groupon and Living Social.

But those who can't, or won't, pay to play are faced with the increasingly daunting challenge of having to drive online performance via organic methods. Ironically, most seem chipper about their prospects of attracting an audience, or, at worst, garnering a few thousand extra clicks through search engine referrals. If only they knew the truth. Not only are millions of sites and sources now competing for users' shrinking time and attention, but according to online marketing service Optify, the top three unpaid positions on page one of Google search results receive 58.4% of all clicks. Websites that appear on page two? Try an average of 1.5%.

The harsh reality: If you make it, chances are, they still won't come. Nonetheless, citing common catchphrases like "content is king" and "great content" as the secret to success, too many entrepreneurs go willingly to the slaughter. The real trick to succeeding online? Designing everything to be shared and creating material of such uniqueness and arresting value that audiences can't help but stop in their tracks, and actively feel compelled to seek it out or pass it along. In other words, whether marketing to smaller B2B channels or larger consumer audiences, suddenly today, every company is in the publishing business.

Note that success is often fleeting, enhancing organic search results won't happen overnight, and unless original content's both striking and substantive, you can blog and tweet until you're blue in the face with little result. One-hit wonders are all too common too: A single breakout smash may provide a brief spike in traffic, but long-term sustainability's another matter entirely. Regardless, there's never been a better time to build a marketing strategy that cost-effectively leverages the power of social media and the Internet. Following are five easy ways for any enterprise to boost online traffic, improve SEO and possibly go viral in the process.

1 Original Articles – Writing about internal initiatives, changes in corporate leadership and breaking news is necessary, but often of little interest to casual observers. Want to secure a meaningful slice of readers' time? As in business, offer something of lasting value in exchange. Original essays, how-to articles, tip sheets, checklists, guidebooks and interviews that offer instructional learning, new methods for tackling problems, insight into best practices and/or access to industry leaders' singular perspectives all make a good starting point.

For maximum impact, build content around popular search engine keywords, recurring questions and industry memes, and design stories to stay evergreen and relevant by excising terms or references that might date them. Note that less is more online as well: Be short and succinct, summarize wherever possible, and instantly grab readers with arresting headlines, bold statements and an authoritative voice. Humor and unique, catchy hooks (e.g. "5 Ways to Torture and Infuriate Your Employees," "The Wrong Way to Downsize," etc.) may prove helpful ways to instantly draw a crowd.

Time investment aside, online clips are minimally expensive and easy to generate, and provide a more empathetic way to brand company representatives and highlight their expertise than official marketing pieces. Storytelling may not seem like your firm's forte, but between marketing, PR, sales and mission statements, consider – it's what all commercial firms already do each and every day.

2 Audio and Video Podcasts – Barriers to entering the online broadcasting business are lower than ever. Armed with a portable digital video camera ($100-$600), USB microphone ($20-$200) and a spare hour of time, anyone can create compelling shows of short- or extended-length format. Best kept under 3 minutes (video series) or 5-15 minutes (audio tapings) in length, it's easy to record behind-the-scenes footage from your office, making-of style documentaries, product demos, customer testimonials, webinars, Q&As, panel discussions and more.

From uniquely-branded video programs ("Engineering 101") to customized training segments ("Launch Your Leadership Career") and exclusive sit-downs ("An Interview with Seth Godin"), you'd be amazed how quickly content can be built and distributed. Even a simple webcam can provide a ready vehicle for recording revealing op-eds, offering answers to pressing industry questions and assembling powerful distance learning sessions, as well as provide the added upside of helping customers put a face to your enterprise. All should be further stamped with your brand's logo, prominently feature business contact information and be promoted via online film aggregators like **YouTube**, **Vimeo** and **Metacafe**.

It's also vital that users be allowed to pass links along and embed (read: screen and share) them on their own websites, as well as be able to download and access audio recordings through popular online distribution services such as **iTunes** and **Podcast.com**.

3 Blogs, Forums and Online Communities – Your company wouldn't be in business if it didn't employ leading subject matter experts in a chosen field. A simple way to build trust, cement credibility and grow both reach and renown: Allow customers ready access to these individuals, and the hard-won knowledge they possess. Similarly, courtesy of their own education and experiences, customers may have additional insights, input and suggestions that they're happy to share with colleagues and peers.

You can tap into a wellspring of ideas, and prospective publishing material, by providing all with blogs, newsgroups, communities, message boards and other open forums where dialogue and ideas are readily exchanged. Not only do such solutions foster creativity and discussion, provide enhanced user support and allow prospective partners or buyers to communicate with and grow trust in internal stakeholders. They also provide a two-way channel for conversation that helps you get to better know your customers, comprehend their needs and stay on top of breaking trends or areas of interest.

From guest posts to user comments, polls, crowdsourced initiatives and regularly-updated columns or community spotlights, such contributions don't just add value to your efforts. They also serve the added benefit of providing ongoing activity and new material that keeps search engines crawling through, and users regularly clicking on, your website.

4 Charts, Diagrams and Infographics – Everyone loves a good Top 10 list or eye-opening survey result. But even more compelling are visually rich pieces such as charts, diagrams and infographics, which make data easy for anyone to understand and digest at a glance.

Eye-catching and easily shareable, cartoon, hand-drawn or computer-illustrated representations of customer preferences, buying habits or population distributions can be a powerful tool for communicating complex data in seconds. They also provide perfect fuel for sound bites ("80% of women now buy beauty accessories online!"), conversation starters and additional media mentions.

Fun facts and especially interesting or one-of-a-kind information, if positioned correctly ("Surveys show 5 in 10 Americans are abandoning cable for online video"), won't just draw audiences' attention. They may also provide a ready platform for publicity that leads to added national newspaper, magazine, radio and TV coverage as well.

5 Books, Hints, Tip Sheets and Online Guides – Everyone has a problem that needs solving: That's why small businesses exist. Providing expert advice, hints, strategies and answers to perennial problems is an excellent way to establish yourself as a leading industry source, gain media exposure and ensure that attention accrues to your company's efforts. Short and sweet summaries – 5 Ways to Increase ROI (Return on Investment), Essential Rules for Project Management, Modern Sales Secrets, etc. – work well for viral pass-along. More extensive manuscripts such as self-published books or reference guides can also heighten user takeaway, and help to establish credentials, build an audience and generate buzz.

Given the ability to digitally circulate all as PDFs; sharable online slideshow presentations; or eBook volumes playable on eReaders, computers, smartphones and tablet PCs such as the iPhone, iPad, Mac, PC or Kindle, doing so is incredibly inexpensive. While you may opt to charge for full or more detailed manuscripts, at least a small initial installment (e.g. an executive summary or sample chapter) should always be given away free. Just be certain to include information of value in the volume. Documents may be easy to forward with a retweet or Facebook Like. But customers are looking for thought leadership, not blatant advertisements, and won't have an interest in passing along a glorified sales pitch.

Sidebar: 5 Ways to Grow Your Business Overnight

It's a fundamental paradox for small business owners: How do you expand your revenues, grow market share and maintain optimum production and service levels without disrupting cash flow or sending operations into a tailspin? Thankfully, even for the most time-, money- or manpower-deprived entrepreneur, a wealth of apps, gadgets and online solutions exists that can help you broaden your reach without biting off more than you can chew. Looking to give your business a sudden boost of upward momentum? Try the following five high-tech tools and services, all of which could potentially prove vital resources in your ongoing fight to score more customers and send profits soaring.

1 **Build an Online Presence** – Need a professional-looking website, but don't have the time, cash or technical know-how to get started? Try **Onepager**, which makes it possible for beginners to establish an attractive online presence in no time flat. Using the site, business owners simply type their company name, tagline and body text into a number of preexisting templates, to which photos and visual styling can be added. A point-and-click interface further makes it easy to introduce newsletter signups, service rundowns, social media links and contact information. Once complete, the site helps you register a domain name, monitor customer behavior and otherwise enjoy the benefits of marketing to the online world. Providers like **Yahoo!** and **1&1** also offer easy off-the-shelf solutions.

2 **Secure Venture Capital** – Have the perfect idea for a new electronic gadget or restaurant chain, but lack the funds to quit your day job, let alone mass-produce consumer products? Do what today's smartest entrepreneurs do: Beg strangers for spare change. Crowdsourced funding sites such as **Kickstarter**, **RocketHub** and **IndieGogo** let you post details of your dream projects, complete with colorful descriptions, photos and videos, then source pledges from the general public. Rather than equity, investors typically receive personalized or product-based incentives for their kindness (e.g., a $5 donation nets a copy of the movie you helped fund's DVD, while $500 scores a personal thank you call from the director). Group seed capital programs such as **Grow VC** and fundraising platforms like **Crowdrise** may also prove a handy alternative to romancing fickle angel investors or handing over 30% of your company for minimal return.

3 **Start Taking Credit Card Payments** – From everyday consumers to major corporations, many customers prefer to pay via credit card. Letting them do so on-demand using a solution like **Square**, which lets you connect a plastic card reader accessory to your iPhone, iPad, iPod Touch or Android mobile device isn't just simple and convenient. It also makes good business sense, allowing you to instantly swipe their American Express, Visa, MasterCard and Discover and secure down payments, project milestones and up-front advances on the spot. Charging a single 2.75% flat fee on each transaction, and letting you setup custom inventories of items with personalized photos, names and prices, it can streamline and simplify billing for businesses of all sizes.

4 Land Free Publicity – Every entrepreneur dreams of making headlines or enjoying time in the spotlight. Help a Reporter Out (**HARO**) offers the opportunity to do so in seconds – and without spending a single dime on marketing or advertisement. A matchmaking service that pairs journalists with subject matter experts, simply submit your name and email to receive a daily newsletter from members of the media who need commenting sources. Think you're the perfect fit to field calls for a professional organizer or whiz in the field of cloud computing? Just respond to the queries that show up in your Inbox, and you could find yourself quoted everywhere from CNN to The New York Times.

5 Create a Custom Virtual Store – The most direct way to put e-commerce to work: Add an attractive online storefront capable of effortlessly handling myriad payment solutions that's chock-full of must-have goods. Multiple options from **Goodsie** to **Shopify**, **Yahoo!** and **Volusion** and **BigCommerce** can help, making it possible to set up both basic solutions that require minimal to no programming, and more complex and sophisticated virtual bazaars. Note that while it's tempting to go big on features and selection here, the first-time builder is advised to keep things simple. Start by staying focused on practicality, convenience and popular high-margin goods, then expand organically, rather than risking overcomplicating your user interface or overwhelming shoppers with frivolous alternatives.

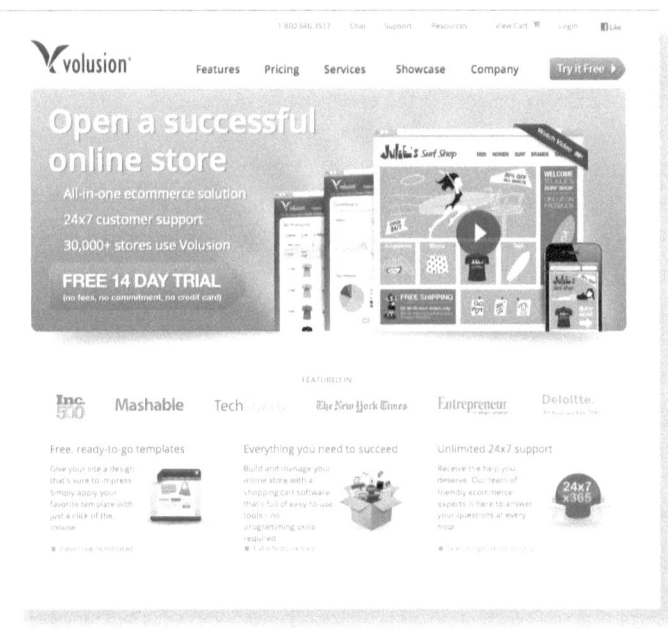

Several off-the-shelf solutions let you grow your business
by opening an online store.

Chapter 5
CROWDSOURCING AND MINIMUM VIABLE PRODUCT: MARKETING IN ACTION

Cult favorite video game developer Double Fine recently shocked investors by raising over **$1 million in 24 hours** on **Kickstarter** for its new adventure game, despite the genre's supposed death. This has led critics to speculate that crowdsourcing isn't just the hottest new thing to happen to startups and small business owners since Apple's App Store; it may also present tomorrow's most promising new source of venture capital and angel investment.

From both research and ROI perspectives, the model makes sense. Why spend years building a better widget when you can instead find and fund tomorrow's next million-dollar idea simply by asking potential customers? Crazy? Not so much. Wasting thousands on research and development up-front, then manufacturing thousands of unproven goods, hoping that they'll actually align with market needs years hence is now an unnecessary approach. Through **crowdsourcing** fundamentals — requesting feedback or recruiting help from public donors via open calls for assistance — you can gauge demand for and create bankable products from day one. That's what entrepreneurs call risk mitigation.

Under current business models, creators can only make educated guesses as to what consumers will buy and how much. By letting shoppers fund only ideas they like best, you know exactly what to create, and in what quantities. Repositioning up-front spends more heavily around development vs. marketing, crowdsourcing allows you to deliver a high-quality product that essentially sells itself. Better still, pre-orders provide working capital to fuel production, and donors feel more emotionally invested in the end result.

To start the process, create just enough design samples, documents and drawings of your product or service to convey its unique selling points. Then, build short two- to five-minute videos that highlight key features and introduce team members and mission statements. Doing so promotes viewer empathy, attractively showcases core concepts and provides a user-friendly platform for sharing your elevator pitch on social media.

When summarizing your product or service, discuss no more than three to four main benefits. Include short, bulleted text descriptions, screenshots, photos and 90-second maximum film clips to dive deeper into supporting topics. And don't forget to dress for success. Regardless of available capital, always double down on visual presentation: People tend to judge on first impressions, and a picture's worth a thousand words.

Also worth noting: From an investor's perspective, working prototypes and vertical slices are far more convincing showpieces than tech demos, sketches and sunny PowerPoint presentations. Therefore, when possible, always use text, mock-ups and prototypes to showcase proposals before public announcement.

Equally important as pre-production and marketing is defining required funding levels, broken into tiers to attract spenders of all budgets. Also, assign associated rewards to each.

Payouts can be physical ($50 nets a copy of the DVD and signed poster) or personal ($500 earns you an executive producer credit and thank you call from the director). It's important to remember that in the wake of the JOBS Act's recent passage, current rules and **regulations** regarding raising money via crowdfunding have yet to be fully defined. Therefore, payouts for crowdfunded, non-qualified investors will, for the most part, take the form of tangible returns, like the aforementioned DVDs. In other words, money donated must essentially amount to pre-ordering future products or services.

Either way, the more value-adds, the merrier. Lest you feel stingy here, remember: They're ultimately cheaper than giving up a piece of your company.

After building presentation materials, you can introduce your designs to the world through your website, or via the following services:

Kickstarter
IndieGogo
RocketHub
33Needs
Spot.us
8BitFunding
Grow VC
Ulule
Community Funded
CrowdCube
Peerbackers
Microryza

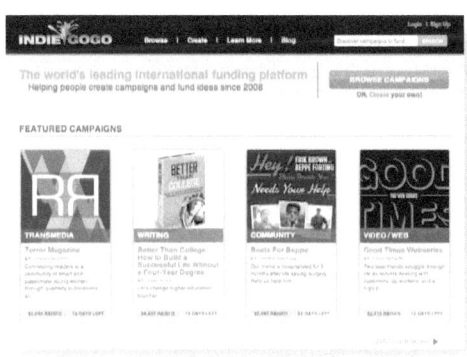

Online funding solutions now offer a viable alternative to seeking angel investment or raising venture capital.

Such online hubs act as both product showroom and public forum, where everyday buyers greenlight projects by voting with their wallets. The beauty: You own the end-product, minus any optional payments or royalties awarded to collaborators or contributors who've submitted original designs for inclusion. Profits from every sale, starting with the first one, help keep the lights on and new ideas flowing.

Win or lose, you not only retain all rights to your creations – you've also begun generating buzz for them and connecting with potential backers and fans.

Crowdsourcing's Partner-in-Success: Minimum Viable Product Theory

Of course, crowdsourcing goes hand-in-hand with today's increasingly popular minimum viable product (MVP) theory, a business strategy which advocates shipping smaller and more polished, yet less expansive and robust products more rapidly. Using its principles, businesses are able to rightsize products or services, bring them to market faster and more quickly generate stable income that can be reinvested into new iterations. Unlike crowdsourcing, MVP theory doesn't ask consumers for funds; it does, however, provide considerable opportunity to solicit feedback and generate excitement among smaller target groups.

According to advocates, it's far preferable to produce a less complex product that's built around a few artfully-realized features versus spending time and money on a far-reaching venture that tries to be all things to all people. By doing so, proponents say, you're able to produce sharper results on tighter turnaround, offer more timely responses to market developments, and bring cash in the door faster, allowing for healthier, more organic growth. Moreover, once on the market, initial products can be used as an interactive focus test unto themselves, providing the chance to source consumer feedback that can be directly incorporated into future iterations.

Here are a few hints, tips and strategies for designing a product around this philosophy.

1 **Plan Extensively Up-Front and Keep Production Cycles Manageable** – When scoping out a product and plotting a production calendar, by all means strive to innovate and push boundaries. However, a lot of companies undeniably kill their products through over-ambitious designs – a problem more commonly known as "feature creep," or trying to cram in too much. One product can't hope to please everyone though, and focus produces enhanced results. It's far better to serve a niche with a brisk, but polished product with a handful of innovations than it is to produce an incredibly complex product that does many things poorly.

Before entering active production, make certain to trim every bit of fat from concepts and designs, and allot extra time for building and testing prototypes that offer a vertical slice, or working sample, of the end product. This will allow you to quickly get a sense of how well concepts are coming together, create a working demo that's ready to wow onlookers, and ultimately produce a clean, polished product that makes consumers happy and gets them talking. Be sure to source customer feedback as you go too, so that you can make adjustments to product designs and craft marketing strategies accordingly.

2 **Release in Parts Versus One Big Whole**– Spending upwards of 12 months to develop a grand-scale product means that you're taking a huge gamble. The virtual equivalent of reading tea leaves and hoping you'll correctly divine where the market's headed months hence, you might as well throw darts at a board and hope they'll land on the correct guesstimate. Stakes are higher than ever today for those speculating on cultural zeitgeists as well. Fail to accurately interpret market forecasts, and your product effectively exists in limbo burning overhead for no good reason, only to flop when it's eventually released.

Instead of attempting to project so far out with ambitious designs, consider releasing more limited versions of your product in waves over the course of the same time period. That way, consumers can have access to the product sooner rather than later. This allows you to discern if a project's connecting out of the gate at less expense, start the process of brand building and bring in revenue streams more rapidly that can help fund future projects. Moreover, a more piecemeal release schedule makes it far easier to respond to breaking developments in the marketplace, and tailor future versions of your product around direct fan feedback.

Too many entrepreneurs spend millions up-front creating lavish websites, apps and services that hinge on consumers pressing a single button or answering a specific call to action. As MVP strategies illustrate, perhaps it's wiser to see if you can cause any action whatsoever first before committing to thousands of man-hours of production, or piling more expensive functionality on the back-end.

3 Expand Only as Progress Dictates – It's important to get a polished, functional version of your product into the public eye as quickly as possible. But from there, you should also make a point of growing organically according to actual cash flow, and criticism and compliments from consumers. Expanding too fast or launching a huge product with a "bang" can potentially overwhelm your financial wherewithal or overwhelm the customer. Instead, it's often smarter to grow at a slow and steady pace so you don't needlessly inflate head count or monthly burn, and give a product the chance to evolve and find its core audience.

Too many companies start with an overambitious plan which they're pre-committed to adhere to, or push too far too fast in the hope of growing rapidly to meet investors' expectations. The wiser goal: Work to build a small, loyal fanbase and stable recurring revenues, then reinvest in expanding your product and company. Once stability's been established, you can see what's working and adjust strategic roadmaps and plans for expansion or acquisition accordingly. Military theorist Carl von Clausewitz once observed that "no plan survives contact with the enemy." As battle-hardened executive generals leading their troops to war well know, being flexible and able to turn on a dime is crucial to survival, today more so than ever.

Sidebar: 7 High-Tech Strategies for Business Survival

From Apple to Facebook and Google, technology titans have quickly become the darlings of the modern business world. But like scrappy young startups such as Flipboard and Pinterest, their success isn't solely rooted in online innovations and cutting-edge electronic advancements. It's also founded in basic management and marketing principles that every entrepreneur can learn from.

Looking to model your startup or small business after today's top industry legends? Relax – it doesn't take a star-studded IPO to follow in their footsteps. Following are five key insights that any firm can glean from today's most successful gadget, app and software makers alike.

1 Treat Any Business Like a Service – Gone are the days of fire-and-forget products and services, especially for those operating in high-tech fields like apps and software development. The lesson here: Once your core product's on the market, whether it's a cutting-edge CRM platform, real-time inventory solution or even just a neighborhood legal or accounting practice, you can't simply operate on cruise control. In this day and age, staying on top of emerging topics/trends and potential business opportunities requires that you forge a direct and ongoing relationship with your customers in order to remain relevant.

To take advantage of the heightened insight and awareness the shift to a service-based model brings, first establish running dialogue with your key constituents – even if they're just the regulars who patronize your restaurant or bar. Afterwards, iterate and introduce changes regularly, reacting to feedback that customers provide. New dinner specials and custom-packaged appliance upgrades may not sound like sexy wares to prototype and experiment with. But mixing things up can help you see how customers respond, and provide invaluable information on variables like pricing, packaging, presentation, usability and consumption patterns.

By proactively taking steps to understand customers' needs and specific problems they're looking to solve, you skip random guesswork and gain the opportunity to smartly and organically expand product lines, service offerings or value-added components. Succeed or fail with individual offerings, rapid iteration will help you stay on top of changing markets. Similarly, by conversing with shoppers and playing to their desires, you'll not only generate new and potentially recurring sources of revenue. You'll also present a ready excuse to keep customers buzzing, thereby constantly staying top of mind and relevant.

2 Perpetually Prototype, Update and Refine – According to social game maker Zynga, "good enough" is the new "perfect" and constant iteration the new norm. Per smash hits like FarmVille and Adventure World, enhanced and expanded upon daily based on user analytics, prototyping isn't just a research tool – done publicly, it can actually be a profitable business.

Letting entrepreneurs quickly gauge consumer reaction, rapid product or service rollouts don't just streamline development compared with full-scale launches by trimming excess features. They also cut costs, improve cash flow, generate ongoing buzz and allow for better market response times. Coupled with extensive data mining, the practice can keep your business from wasting time and resources by rightsizing based on consumer response, and improve overall conversion rates.

Whether launching larger initiatives in parts or simply teasing diners with limited-time blue plate specials, consider. It may pay greater dividends in the long run to fail rapidly and often, and grow more organically through ongoing iteration. Sometimes, less is truly more.

Also important to note: Make certain you're capturing data every step of the way. Valuable information includes not only end-user feedback, but information on how your product is being monetized, when and how consumers are using it, primary reasons for purchase, how price changes affect sales and more as well.

Repeat it to yourself until it sinks in – you can never have too much information. Gather and decipher as much of it as you possibly can to fine-tune new upgrades, service offerings, deals, specials, promotions and/or future releases, and constantly respond to market feedback. Think of customers and prospective clients as the most sophisticated and opinionated market focus group you could ever meet. Knowing this, it's imperative to create feedback loops both active (respond to our survey) and passive (tracking every click made on your online storefront) at multiple touchpoints to mine this data, and use the insights they provide to your advantage.

3 Be Objective and ROI-Focused with Concepts – The days of speculation and idle tinkering are over: In an age of endless competition and cost-cutting, every feature products and services offer must add tangible value. For entrepreneurs, that means having to be brutal – and brutally objective – when assessing new concepts or milestone additions.

Whether financial in nature, or a means of boosting engagement and usability, you can't afford to waste resources or manpower. Just ask the increasing number of startups hoping to secure venture capital through public donations on crowdfunding sites like Kickstarter, RocketHub or IndieGogo. You can pitch until you're blue in the face – if the idea doesn't convince customers, it never even moves beyond the concept phase. Harsh? Perhaps, but it's better to experience a reality check before manufacturing thousands of units that unexpectedly spend years moldering in your warehouse.

To this extent, don't spend the time and money necessary to add a feature to your product or service line unless that feature adds significant value. Introducing social media elements to your company's creations, for instance, gives people a chance to interact with one another (say, by sharing user reviews and video dedications), and also gives them a reason to sign in over and over again and keep clicking. The longer those users hang around, the more likely they are to spend money on microtransactions, add-ons, upgrades or time-saving features, or become familiar and enamored with your brand.

The key takeaway here: Do extensive due diligence and weigh choices carefully when considering every option on the table during the preproduction, build-out and deployment phases. Knowing when to pull the plug on projects, and not waste time, money and manpower, is also every bit as important as knowing when to take risks or add new options.

4 Give It Away Free and Then Upcharge – From Spotify to Dropbox, Amazon Cloud Drive to Pandora, the smartest thing many of today's high-tech leaders do is let you steal their software. These so-called "freemium" offerings minimize user friction by making products free to download and install. Effortless for users to obtain on myriad mobile devices, the practice promotes mass trial and sharing, and provides a showcase for advanced features and add-ons, available for optional back-end purchase or subscription.

Paired with sticky experiences that prompt ongoing interaction (regular news delivery, streaming music, etc.), the practice promotes constant brand awareness and value reinforcement. Some big spenders (known as "whales") may even pay many times over what they would on a single-shot retail purchase. Be forewarned, however – conversion rates often dip as low as 2-3%, making volume plays essential here.

Creations should always intrigue as many people as possible and allow hands-on trials with the fewest number of required steps, links or actions. The more a person has to click, type, tap or plug in personal information to access a product or service, the more opportunities they have to lose interest in the item or opportunity. For software, apps and high-tech solutions, this includes taking system requirements into account, too: The less hardware features or minimum power your program requires out of a PC, smartphone or tablet, the larger the number of individuals that can enjoy it.

5 **Try the Hands-Off Approach** – Apple's App Store undoubtedly enjoyed a boost from the popularity of the iPhone, iPod and iPad. But its real success can be attributed to thousands of enterprising external software developers. The lesson here: Rather than lording over proprietary solutions, sometimes it pays to empower end-users, and provide more open platforms and solutions.

Relinquishing control is often anathema to corporations. But whether offering customers the chance to personalize brand experiences by simply inserting themselves into virtual film posters or creating custom software tools which piggyback on patented technologies, consider. Rather than take the draconian approach, your business may enjoy greater prosperity by establishing basic ground rules, then giving partners a little freedom to color between the lines.

Accordingly, wherever possible, brands and content providers should always give end-users the tools to expand or create their own spin upon an app, service, product line or software platform (even if you're just providing the chance for fans to insert themselves into advertisements on Facebook, or make YouTube-ready remixes of favorite soda jingles). You can see this philosophy reflected in the success of the Android Market, which has enjoyed steady growth thanks to the support of thousands of enterprising third-party developers. Blogging solutions have also benefited from similar approaches, e.g., WordPress, which has quickly become a favorite with web designers thanks to a constant supply of new plugins provided by amateur and professional creators alike.

Naturally, fans should also be provided ample incentive for sharing content and passing unique creations along. In the case of popular social games such as Empires & Allies and The Sims Social, the ability to unlock bonus items, share advancements or recruit help to accomplish goals makes for a good reason for Facebook players to pass game recommendations along to friends. Word-of-mouth remains a powerful marketing tool, especially when backed by the collective creativity and imagination of the online world at large.

6 **Change, Reinvent and Add Ongoing Value** – Little-known fact: Facebook's IPO was fueled by more than glib one-liners and narcissistic profile shots. Rather, it's the social network's constant willingness to reinvent and grow value-added content by introducing new features and services or boosting opportunities for interaction that's powered its meteoric growth.

At a base level, beyond addressing changing market tastes, each update tracks user response and – whether by sharing Timeline updates or song selections – provides added reason to stay logged in and clicking. But besides improving virality, the practice also provides invaluable data on usage and spending habits, helping enhance customer service and targeted advertising placements. (A practice further espoused by frontrunners like Amazon and Zappos.) If your business isn't taking steps to evolve, enhance and create dialogue with customers today, it's ill-poised to compete tomorrow.

Pop culture, technological innovations and best practices never stay stationary, and you can't count on them to do so if you're investing the time and money necessary to build a modern product or service. Imagine spending two years developing a cutting-edge new social network, only to discover that micro-blogging or location-based community solutions have become the hottest new trend amongst technorati just before your finished product releases. Today's most successful products and brands – be they high-tech or otherwise – succeed because they quickly improve upon old ideas, or adapt to emerging trends, by actively listening to and acting upon user feedback.

Wherever possible, take advantage of the market's changing tastes, evolving standards and new innovations by maintaining agile production cycles and rightsizing projects/products. That way you can respond to new developments quickly, and effectively parallel industry and cultural shifts as they happen.

7 Make Customers Paramount – If you have an ongoing dialogue with your customers and data on where they're spending their time and money, then you know what proverbial levers you can pull to adjust variables like sales, revenue, lead generation and overall conversions. But you can't afford to ignore the basic building block that continues to serve so many industry-leading firms from Amazon to Zappos well: An emphasis on customer service.

Today, more so than ever, thousands of options and competitors are just a click away. So whether building custom home furnishings, on-demand food delivery services or photo-sharing applications, remember: The customer is always right. If he or she isn't solving day-to-day problems, having fun, participating in a community, sharing ideas or otherwise finding reason to stick around, be forewarned: Regardless of how good, well-informed or innovative your business is, it's liable to be abandoned in favor of rivals in record time.

Chapter 6
SALES AND BUSINESS DEVELOPMENT:
THE INSIDE SECRETS

E very individual in business, whether employed full-time or a prospective entrepreneur, wants to make themselves stand out and be more bankable. But at the same time, many fail to observe several simple business strategies that can help them do just that.

Some strategems may seem like common sense, but don't be fooled. From custom-tailoring every pitch around recipients' latest needs to doing a little advance online research about your potential partners and clients, you'd be amazed at the difference they make.

Basic in nature, but capable of having a big impact, the following insights can get you on any decision-maker's good side and make both yourself and your company more marketable in seconds flat.

Research Your Target

Take a tip from modern hiring managers, who have a much faster and more affordable way to perform background checks than ever: A moment's online search can provide you with a wealth of background information.

While some may jest that punching other parties' or firms' names into Google is tantamount to stalking, outside of rare cases where taken to an extreme, it's really reconnaissance. A brief query is often all it takes to discover important information regarding a business and recent happenings that may affect any deals or pitches (i.e. sudden internal restructurings, new partnerships or emerging legislation) you're presenting. Similarly, you may be able to glean vital insight into key contacts, including their general approach to doing business, or any current professional mandates and initiatives they're tasked with spearheading. (At the very least, you should get a sense as to whether you should talk sports or finance when making small talk.) If it seems shady or underhanded, consider: Today, chances are more likely than not that the HR department took a good look at your Twitter feed, Facebook profile and personal blog before ever handing an employment contract over.

Pause for a moment and contemplate the facts. While one commonly has a sense of a company's scale of operations and what its brand name stands for, how frequently do you know exactly what factors and variables are impacting its business or decision-making process on a day-to-day basis? Likewise, how often do you really dig deep in terms of background research to understand just whom you're hoping to collaborate with, as well as their basic outlook and mindset? Press releases, interviews, industry profiles, bylined op-eds, even personal websites – any fragment of information lingering on the far corners of the Internet can give clues to the personality, interests and inclinations of third parties. Similarly, all can provide understanding into a company's present position, including current marching orders; new growth and opportunity areas; and the firm's general philosophy and attitude towards certain ventures at said moment in time.

In the same vein, it's also imperative that you're wholly versed in who occupies what role, and where, in your particular industry food chain at any given second. After all, you never know whom you'll accidentally run into, or how surprised and delighted they'll be when you not only recognize them, but also recall details of their recent exploits. Keeping abreast of personnel comings and goings can also provide a sense of where fresh points of contact may have opened. (A recently-hired marketing manager, for example, may be more open to working with new vendors than one who's used the same entrenched partners for 10 years.) Clever individuals can even make a point of monitoring comings and goings as these notables as they speak at conferences, address professional trade groups or give training workshops. Keeping abreast of such opportunities may help you gain the chance to connect with them in-person, and thereby enjoy the benefit of being more than another faceless email correspondent, or grabbing a moment of their time that would otherwise be unobtainable.

Studying ahead can also help you avoid potential gaffes, including trying to sell someone on something they don't need, let alone in the wrong manner. Moreover, it gives you an immediate advantage, as people typically find themselves more willing to open up and relate to those who take an active interest in their professional or personal accomplishments. Don't be disingenuous about it, and simply make passing conversation or idly name-drop – sycophants are easy to spot and always off-putting. The moral of the story: To really succeed, you've got to show those you're selling to that you genuinely care about their business, and let it show, via both words and actions, even before the relationship is officially consecrated.

> **Pro Tip** – Having trouble remembering someone's name? Ask for a copy of their latest business card early into the conversation, under the auspices that you'd like to have their most recent contact info handy. And in a boardroom situation, simply take these cards and keep them lined up in front of you facing each corresponding individual – voila, instant CliffsNotes.

First Give, Then Get

Per bestselling book The 48 Laws of Power, "If you're miserly by nature, you'll never go beyond a certain limit – only generous souls attain greatness." Or, as budding entrepreneurs would be well advised to note, a single free drink or second's kindness can often take you further than an entire year's worth of emails and cold calls.

Don't be afraid to make the gesture of paying for that lunch, or lending your 5 o'clock meeting your cell phone so they can call home and let the wife know that they'll be late. The act of offering such amenities alone signifies good manners, communicates a certain level of care and, in the case of comped meals, reinforces that you're not hurting for business. Picking up the tab for a flight or soy latte may seem pointless, or act of needless braggadocio. But by helping to build trust and camaraderie, the friendly gesture could come back to you 20X over in future dividends, if it means getting on vendors' good sides, or establishing greater rapport with a key contact.

As is increasingly evident from today's growing focus on generating short-term results and immediate performance over building long-term relationships, the realm of business becomes harsher and more distant with each passing day. When you take 15 minutes out of your hectic schedule to meaningfully sit down and listen to someone; answer a query seeking advice or insight at no personal gain; or simply forward a professional acquaintance's name to a potential business partner sans prompting, it can make a lasting impression. As illustrated in Chapter 1, it helps to think of every day as an interview, and treat others with respect and dignity, regardless of potential gain. If for no other reason, realize that people are constantly changing jobs, industries and firms. You never know when potential opportunities may come knocking courtesy of a grateful contact that you did a small kindness for or made an unexpected impression upon.

Again, you can't fake being forthright: Gestures have to be undertaken honestly, and at personal expense. (Say, during a time when your company's not hosting an open bar or free lunch.) It also pays to be vigilant: Human nature being what it is, even a single negative experience can color the tone of future interactions, no matter how much time you've previously invested in building a relationship. From refusing to comp parking to promising a trusted freelancer piles of work, then having to pull it at the last minute, realize – people remember these instances, and take them to heart. To some, it may be "just business," but the same principle they teach in elementary school – "do unto others as you would have done unto you" – also applies in the commercial world. Don't believe in karma? Fair enough. But don't forget: A former associate you've alienated can easily end up heading up similar programs for one of your mainstay clients thanks to a sudden job move, and yesterday's disgruntled employee may become tomorrow's rival CEO.

Bearing this in mind, when it comes to personal branding (and your reputation is indeed your brand, so treat it with equal care), you can't afford to shortchange yourself. Investments needn't be strictly monetary in nature either. A simple note to see how someone's doing; a friendly smile and cup of coffee during a harried convention; or just an offhand referral to a prospective employer when they're between jobs can provide a potentially huge windfall tomorrow. After all, wouldn't you want others to show you the same professional courtesy?

> **Pro Tip** – Operating on an especially tight budget? Consider whether there's a cost-affordable alternative – e.g. less complex solution, referral to an alternate resource, etc. – that you can provide. While you can't always afford time- and money-wise to assist with every query that comes across your desk, you may still be able to make the other party's life easier. Case in point: Just because your

graphic design firm can't tackle a job under certain constraints doesn't mean you couldn't point an associate towards equally capable independent contractors so that they don't find themselves back at square one.

Employ Patience, Persistence, and Personality

Haste makes waste, as they say, and tends to sink even the most promising deals – the more desperate you seem to strike a bargain, the less likely you are to land it. To this extent, a certain respectable degree of restraint and aloofness is required to intrigue and land any prospect. Eager as many entrepreneurs and salesman are to "close the big deal," they miss a fundamental truth. Clients need to feel like such opportunities are routine for you, and, by proxy, that they're in good, experienced hands who know how to effectively handle such opportunities.

So take a deep breath and relax. Experienced salespeople know that self-assurance, poise under pressure and the ability to think fast will get you further than long-winded speeches and high-impact PowerPoint presentations. Likewise, it's those who address hard questions head-on, not dance around them or stammer out scripted responses, which inspire the most empathy and confidence in potential partners. Of course, appearance counts somewhat too: Since most people tend to accept things at face value, always dress to impress, and come ready to get right to the point. Ultimately though, if you want to close a deal, you need to be able to show a proven track record; point to directly relatable examples and case studies that speak to your expertise; and be prepared to deftly field any question put your way.

If it helps you to stay frosty, realize: Never take it personal. Numerous firms staffed with equally eager and ambitious talent are always bidding for the same RFPs. Some rivals will inevitably resonate better with different decision makers, and even on the best days, successful close rates for certain businesses can be as low as 5-15% in various industries. But the good news is as follows. There are always "big" opportunities out there to be had, and if clients don't like what you're selling, it's generally not an issue – your next call can be to their closest half-dozen competitors.

Staying cool, calm and collected isn't just an ideal to aspire to. It's also a necessity in any high-pressure business situation. Regardless of how dismal things truly are, it pays to stay positive. The happier and more together you appear to be, the cheerier and more able you'll be perceived as being by clients and colleagues alike. Likewise, no matter the timeframe you're operating under, even if you absolutely, positively have to make a venture work ASAP, you'll only set yourself up for failure if you go in expecting to close a deal quickly.

A surefire way to torpedo any budding arrangement: Trying to brute force it after a client humbly requests some time to consider their options. Do so, and they'll wonder why you aren't confident enough to provide breathing room, or worse, worry what it is that you have to hide. Similarly, appealing to people's sense of kindness or generosity seldom works in a boardroom scenario. To make headway with a deal in today's ROI-driven corporate culture, you need to illustrate that you've got something the other party wants, and show via measurable results how they can directly benefit from the association.

Naturally, making a convincing case may take weeks and require you to be shuffled between several points of contact until you earn the right to an audience with a key influencer. Take a deep breath, be patient, and keep cracking away at the situation. And remember, everyone's more swamped than ever – radio silence is par for the course. Unless actively prodded from time to time amidst the hustle, bustle and general chaos of daily work schedules, there's scant reason for them to get back to you, unless it relates to solving an immediately-prioritized problem. That said, if you want to save some time when pitching partnerships or deals, it often pays to be brash and reach out to someone high up on the corporate food chain. Oftentimes, an introduction or forward from a higher-ranking executive to a subordinate can save you from spinning your wheels, provide greater visibility or offer a rapid rerouting to a preferred point of contact. Note that taking your case directly to the top may be seen as a breach of etiquette in some firms, though. Nonetheless, in today's connected world, where C-level execs are just a single Facebook friend or LinkedIn introduction away, just as many partners may not mind the gesture or find it a refreshing show of initiative.

Whatever you do when pitching possible new business or partnerships though, make sure you do it with style and personality. It sounds pithy, but you'll never make a splash without rocking the boat. Preoccupied with their own needs and concerns as they are, people will attempt to dismiss both you and your firm and lump you into the same nondescript category as dozens of competitors if allowed to. Pull a 180, and you'll constantly keep them hooked as well as guessing, ensuring that you'll always remain on the tip of their tongue – and near the front of their Rolodex.

> **Pro Tip** – Find a way to stand out. From self-published and -promoted manuscripts to complimentary webinars, instructional video clips or sponsored events, raise the stakes, and your profile, accordingly. Many of these projects – e.g. podcasts and bylined articles – can be executed at little to no cost. These assets can all help speak to your level of performance, creative capabilities and expertise, providing concrete examples to hold in-hand or useful giveaways you can leave behind when pitching. As best-selling author Robert Greene explains, "Everything is judged by its appearance. Be conspicuous at all costs."

Make a Point of Actively Following Up

We all walk a fine line when it comes to follow-up. Moreso than ever today, given sheer levels of distraction, it's imperative that you stay on top of people but not be perceived as overzealous or desperate. Unfortunately, there's no fixed rule here beyond taking cues from the client themselves (e.g. touching base in precisely a week if they request that long to come to a decision). Should you reach out and receive no response, though, we recommend a patterned approach to successive outreach, alternating brief phone calls or emails no more frequently than every three to five days. While there's no hard or fast rule for online etiquette as relates to social networks, no more than a single note on LinkedIn or Facebook (if any at all – oftentimes it's seen as an intrusion on personal space) is typically acceptable. (And generally should be avoided wherever possible, especially as a brief online search is often enough to discern company mailing format – e.g., firstname.lastname@company.com – and individual email addresses.) Likewise, no more than two to three attempts at outreach should be made without response in aggregate.

Either way, get yourself a good calendar, take diligent notes and prepare yourself to deal with rejection: It's not uncommon to see 10, 30 or even 100 or more emails go ignored before a single lead presents itself. Unfortunately, in the sales and business development fields, you have to learn to be thick-skinned. Just remember that the more clients and case studies you add to your resume, the more potential opportunities you'll be able to rope in. If that means doing pro bono or discounted work, or collaborating with charitable organizations and trade groups on a volunteer basis to build a portfolio when getting started, be prepared to take the plunge. Also keep in mind that it's always best to under-promise and over-deliver. Certainly, expectations will always be high – paying clients don't deserve any less. But even for the most experienced of firms, it's crucial to skip the bragging, no matter how successful past ventures have been, and let your work speak for itself.

Pro Tip – Given the time it can take to close deals, aspiring entrepreneurs are advised to have at least one existing client on-hand before launching any venture. A year's worth of expenses should also be in the bank prior to taking the full-time plunge. Even when deals close, expect payments to take longer to process than anticipated by anywhere from 30 to 90 days or more, despite contracts' stated terms. Cash flow is by far the biggest killer of businesses: To help manage intake and outflow, keep at least six months of liquid reserves on-hand to offset monthly overhead.

Chapter 7
LESSONS FROM GUITAR HERO:
MARKETING MISTAKES TO AVOID

Many entrepreneurs dream of being rock stars in their field like Richard Branson and Mark Cuban. But pitfalls are manifold and the limelight sparing – they don't reserve airtime on *Entertainment Tonight* for the stories of the thousands of men and women who failed to achieve similar success in their ventures. To this extent, it's worth examining a case study in how even the most promising of new ventures and industries can go awry when business owners lose sight of key principles like those discussed in Chapter 5. Appropriately, it concerns a pair of would-be legends who, like many headlining acts, imploded soon after rocketing to the top of the charts in their own right: Hard-partying music video games Guitar Hero and Rock Band.

As pop culture fans (and anyone with a teenager in the home) are aware, music and rhythm games like Guitar Hero and Rock Band were once one of the last decade's fastest-growing fields. After peaking at $1.7 billion in annual revenues in 2008, then falling by 46% just one year later though, taking the entire interactive entertainment industry's fortunes with them, they're now a cautionary fable. Not all fun and games, however, you'll find serious lessons in operations, marketing and leadership at the crux of the genre's misfortune that every entrepreneur should know, whatever their professional field. (For deeper insight, you can see ***Music Games Rock: Rhythm Gaming's Greatest Hits of All Time***, a free downloadable book that explores the field's meteoric rise and fall.) A summary of the case study's most pressing takeaways, especially as relates to marketing and sales, follows.

Among the key lessons to be learned:

Differentiate Product Offerings – First came *Guitar Hero*, a performance simulator which let you live out rock 'n roll fantasies by strumming along with songs on a plastic axe. Then Rock Band, which added support for group play, including bass, drum and vocals. Early sequels benefited from token improvements like upping visual quality and adding more music. But later releases, largely indistinguishable, defaulted to minor enhancements for veteran players, i.e. additional multiplayer modes and group harmonies, and failed to offer most consumers tangible value. Charging $99+ per software/hardware bundle (double the then-average video game SRP), despite a growing swell of clones and uniquely-positioned competitors, these attempts to annualize each franchise led to buyer confusion. Lesson Learned: All major product and service upgrades must be paired with one to three major feature additions – especially those offering measurable everyday worth that are easily communicable at a glance.

Don't Oversaturate the Market – Buoyed by the genre's seemingly unstoppable rise, no less than 75 music games were released between 2005 and 2010, including nearly 20 iterations of *Guitar Hero* (*On Tour, Rocks the '80s, Mobile, Smash Hits*, etc.) alone. Not only did new entrants serve to further fragment the market (should you buy *SingStar* or Lips? *Wii Music* or *Rock Revolution*?) and perplex buyers. Many like Green Day: Rock Band also incongruously played to small audience subsets. Not only did shoppers gag at the prospect of buying still more plastic instruments and painfully expensive artist tributes, but reviewers panned many as the overpriced equivalent of downloadable expansion packs – more easily distributed products with better margins. Lesson Learned: Scarcity still commands a premium, and while serving niche markets can be profitable, production and distribution should be rightsized to match.

Be Conservative – Driven by the sale of $100 or more prepackaged sets, executives watched the then-novel music game category's fortunes soar initially. But at the time, direct historical sales comparisons were limited, and the games priced way higher than those in rival genres. Rather than base projections on decades of possible references including minor, less well-known launches, both franchises used a handful of breakout successes specifically tied to plastic instrument sales as touchpoints to found overly optimistic forecasts. When the field's luster inevitably dulled (right as economic woes hit, ironically), the numbers didn't add up. Lesson Learned: Project conservatively and tread lightly in unknown markets, lest you suddenly find yourself scrambling to downscale amidst the pressures of crushing overhead, unsold inventory and rapidly deteriorating cash flow.

Establish a Unique Identity – Despite pioneering the Japanese music game field with 1999 guitar simulator *GuitarFreaks*, publisher Konami watched helplessly as game developer Harmonix's seemingly similarly-styled *Guitar Hero* enjoyed the stateside success that had long eluded it. In response, it launched *Rock Revolution* (which aped Harmonix's own Rock Band) in 2008, yet offered more complex play and no meaningful feature additions to the sound of chirping crickets. Lesson Learned: Success can't simply be aped – whether via aggressive pricing, original features or novel positioning, unique sales points must be established; if a market leader exists, direct battles are suicidal.

Grow Organically – In 2009, Harmonix unleashed ultimate tribute piece *The Beatles: Rock Band*. Backed by MTV's cachet, the world's foremost game developer and history's biggest band, it aimed to extend gaming's reach by appealing to Baby Boomers, and bridge the gap between generations. But despite massive publicity and praise, older audiences remained indifferent, younger listeners less familiar with the band balked, and it struggled to go multiplatinum. Lesson Learned: Rather than grow a market from scratch, it's often smarter financially to speak to an existing audience by addressing their present needs, or identifying a void and filling it.

Go Big or Go Home – Curiously, 2010's largest music game craze was also arguably its dumbest:

A push for more lifelike play in response to critics' claims that games don't resemble playing real instruments. Spurred on by this vocal minority, titles like *Rock Band 3* and *Power Gig* repeated earlier industry mistakes: Promoting teaching aids more than wish fulfillment, and demanding actual skill from players, they steered titles even harder towards niche demographics. Both ultimately failed to perform commercially, while UbiSoft's later 2011 release *Rocksmith*, powered by a real guitar, also followed in their footsteps. Lesson Learned: The loudest opinion isn't always the wisest – and, no matter how novel an approach seems, adding friction to a product's user design or interface will only contract interest, possible sales and your marketing funnel.

Concentrate on What Works – Following *Rock Band 3*'s failure, former owner Viacom jettisoned Harmonix in 2010. But despite dwindling returns at retail, *Rock Band* continued to prove a platinum hit, with over one million people connecting online, even after its so-called downfall, to download new music month. Unsurprisingly for a game its own creator calls "a platform," the series' digital distribution features proved to be far more viable a long-term business than its retail operations ever were. Lesson Learned: Double down on existing profit centers and high-margin growth areas, then expand organically, rather than overreach in hopes of chasing faster growth and expose your enterprise to the high-risk rollercoaster ride of market speculation.

PART 2

PUBLIC RELATIONS
LEVERAGING THE POWER
OF PRESS AND SOCIAL MEDIA

Chapter 8
POWER PR: HOW TO MAKE HEADLINES

It's the dream of every entrepreneur: To see your business' name in lights. But with thousands of companies competing in hundreds of verticals for the same limited number of column inches, blog posts and precious seconds of airtime, let's level – scoring the precious publicity boost that placement in a national newspaper or an influential website can provide isn't easy. Nor, for that matter, is avoiding the trap of becoming yesterday's news.

However, the upside for even the leanest start-ups is that these days, it doesn't take massive marketing and public relations budgets or lavish events to generate serious ink. (Case in point: Our own high-tech consulting firm, <u>TechSavvy</u>, which received dozens of mentions in major media outlets from *Forbes* to FOX News and *USA Today* before it even had a formal website.) Mind you, there's no one simple strategy for breaking into every outlet – each is actually a broad collection of self-contained sections staffed by a unique team of reporters with various backgrounds, interests and needs. But employ the simple tips below, and who knows? You too could soon be making headlines.

1 Get Your Story Straight – Ask yourself: What makes my company unique? Because with countless rivals out there competing for the same space, what's to make an editor choose you out of a sea of faceless competitors? Knowing this, it's imperative that you instantly set yourself apart from the pack in journalists' minds. Look at things from their perspective – they need to immediately identify compelling stories, then condense and translate these gems into digestible nuggets that anyone can enjoy. So start by picking three attributes, or unique sales points, that present your case and weaving them into a compelling narrative, which makes it fast and simple to see where a potential fit lies.

2 Perfect Your Pitch – Decided how you want to present yourself? Great – now brush up on that elevator pitch and figure out how to do it in 30 seconds or less. Because that's roughly the amount of attention you'll get from a journalist if you're lucky, given how under-the-gun today's reporters are given shrinking newsroom staffing levels and a constant deluge of incoming calls and email. The lesson here: Whatever you have to say, keep it short and sweet. Because the second it starts coming out of your mouth, listeners will already be vetting the topic's potential, knowing it'll have to both make sense to and hook readers/viewers in even less time, e.g., two sentences or less.

3 Tailor for Every Outlet – Repeat to yourself until it sinks in: One size does *not* fit all when it comes to pitching media outlets. Every publication effectively has its own singular approach and voice when it comes to covering topics, and actually consists of a collection of numerous smaller vehicles (front-of-book sections, feature wells, etc.) that do so in varied ways. Likewise, every editor and reporter has their own way of tackling these tasks, meaning it pays to read up on and be intimately familiar with both the magazine and specific section you're angling for a spot in. Always bear in mind that different audiences have different needs as well: You wouldn't provide seasoned sales professionals with the same spiel that you would a readership of casual job seekers. By keeping these points in mind and pitching a section and article format that properly aligns with the story you're promoting, you'll avoid being discounted as a poor fit right off the bat.

4 **Prepare Assets in Advance** – Fun fact: Deadlines can be painfully tight in the age of real-time journalism. And inevitably, whether it's high-resolution artwork, product fact sheets or a quick phone call request, you're going to be asked for supporting information or materials on any story pitch. So do yourself a favor: From screen grabs to sample copies and supporting videos, make sure all of these materials are prepared well in advance and are ready to be provided to journalists on tight turnaround. You won't just save yourself the hassle of having to put out a fire when it inevitably ignites. You'll also minimize chances of missing a key opportunity or torching a reporter's trust simply because you couldn't manage to supply a few screenshots, throw up an FTP file transfer or handle another normally easily accommodated task at the last-minute.

5 **Issue Press Releases and Media Advisories** – Press releases and media advisories – simple summaries that outline breaking news announcements or let reporters know that specific experts are available for interview – make an easy, effective way to communicate your sales pitch. Never written one before? Don't sweat it: Dozens of free templates exist online. Once done, assemble a list of media members that you'd like to approach (the more targeted the better), then blast the document out. While chances of receiving an immediate or overwhelming response are often minimal, it still makes a handy reference point should you pique a journalist's interest, making it simple to see what you're offering at a glance. An important rule of thumb here: Always convey your key talking points in the headline, subhead and first two sentences, and include contact info in these documents that includes email addresses and phone numbers. Likewise, be sure to respond with alacrity to any queries that come in.

6 **Follow Up on Correspondence** – Issuing a press release is all well and good, whether via traditional wires or free online services. However, it's only one step in a properly planned PR strategy. Consider how many emails you receive in your inbox on a given day then triple it – that's roughly the amount of information your average reporter is dealing with. Therefore it's imperative that you follow up on initial queries with an email or phone call later once a respectful amount of time has passed and repeat as needed at appropriate intervals. Don't be offended if you don't get a response either. With staffing levels down, deadlines tight and more folks competing for attention then ever, not everything will make the cut, and time-strapped journalists don't always have the bandwidth to send a formal response. Roll with it – with a daily, weekly or even hourly need for breaking news, there's always room to connect on other stories later.

7 **Don't Carpet Bomb Reporters** – When it comes to media outreach, keenly focused efforts yield greater impact than taking a shotgun approach. Accordingly, for each outlet you plan on reaching out to, pick one or two points of contact with the greatest relevancy vs. spamming dozens of editors. That way, you not only minimize the number of touchpoints to keep up with and ensure you can give these individuals the most attention in terms of outreach and follow-up. You also make sure six editors don't show up at an editorial planning meeting ready to propose a "hot new idea" that just coincidentally happens to sound the exact same from every one of them.

8 **Keep Your Promises** – Pitching a "revolutionary new approach to online commerce" or piece of software that promises to "redefine videoconferencing and telecommunications as we know it?" Great – just be certain you've got the goods to back it up, lest journalists feel swindled, underwhelmed or that they've pointlessly wasted hours on a wild goose chase. Likewise, don't promise an exclusive story or breaking interview that you're unable to deliver on or have to cancel at the last minute. Remember: Broadcasters and writers have bosses, external vendors (readers/viewers) and internal stakeholders that they must report to as well, and a limited amount of time and resources to please all parties. Time is precious – be cognizant of what you're offering in return.

9 **Stress Relationship Building** – Stories come and go on a daily basis – people you'll work with at various outlets who effectively act as gatekeepers for each publication's industry-specific coverage, not so much. This being the case, one can't afford to go about wantonly burning bridges, and it's imperative to establish the same healthy working relationship with reporters that you would with anyone you work with day in and day out on a professional basis. As such, it pays to respect media members' opinions. If they don't feel a story is a fit, acknowledge it and move on instead of going for the hard sell. (Hint: It's perfectly OK to ask "why" so you'll be better equipped the next time you have a pitch to field.) Similarly, should they write something you don't agree with, rather than trying to browbeat a correction or apology out of them, be proactive and attempt to balance things out with a future posting. Moral of the story: Think long-term here, and you'll be well on your way to a front-page showing.

10 **Create a Winning Track Record** – In keeping with the aforementioned item, it's vital to be trustworthy, considerate and professional in all dealings with the press. (Doubly so considering that every employee is direct a reflection on the company and brand they represent.) Remember: A publicist's manner, availability and courteousness are always under scrutiny – even when that publicist is also the company's CEO. This doesn't mean you should kiss up to reporters, or can't join them for the occasional drink. Rather, just be approachable and consistent in your performance, and willing to go that extra mile to give everything a personal touch. It's further crucial to be honest and forthcoming, and important to be just as responsive when tackling tough questions as easy ones – that's how you build trust. Likewise, there's no substitute for face-to-face interaction: Often, an on-site visit here or handshake there, regardless of if you're actually pitching something, can help build tremendous empathy, and make all the difference.

The New Rules of Social Networking: A Cautionary Tale

After working diligently to build positive press in all available news outlets, the last thing you want is for your – or an employee's – social networking accounts to scream "unprofessional," "obnoxious" or "offensive." If you've had enough of being besieged by "friends" who pepper your page with crappy dating ads and links to get rich quick schemes, or hearing play-by-play updates about your college roommate's sister's three-legged marmot, chances are your potential clients, customers and media contacts are too. Here are some tips for ensuring that in this new age of virtual enlightenment, your personal communications send the same message as your business communications.

Think Twice – The speed and distance conversation travels may have changed with the rise of real-time online communication, but one thing hasn't: Common sense remains sorely underrated. So no matter how insightful or LOL-worthy your latest epiphany seems, resist the urge to post it immediately, and be sure to stop and think twice before hitting share. Impulse posting can be fun, but it's hardly worth the downsides. Seriously… Does anyone (especially your boss, whom you should know better than to friend in the first place – one word: boundaries) really care to know that (zOMG!) after going six days without bathing after a recent camping trip that you can knock passersby out cold at 10 feet just by lifting an arm?

Nix the Close-Ups – Hey, we lived through the '80s too, which gives us the right to ask: Who dug up the Glamour Shots, dusted off their festering corpse and gave rampant narcissism the green light again? Our best guess: From the smoky-eyed, scantily-clad poses so many of today's webcam users insist on striking in full public view, well… not parents, HR reps or job recruiters. So please, folks, for your poor mother's sake (and career prospects), if nothing else, try and keep those stills PG-rated – plus consider limiting the number of self-portraits cluttering up your wall and photo albums to a maximum of 37.

Fear Commitment – Except with actual real-life pals (you know, those goofy-looking pink blobs you occasionally share an Orange Julius with in meatspace), online exchanges are best kept fleeting. Translation: Don't slather virtual acquaintances' profiles in hot pink stickers or links to questionable content (e.g. YouTube videos of chipmunks square dancing). It may seem cute at the time. But there's nothing like having to scrape someone's petulant blog post or assorted cultural detritus off your wall to make you wonder: "Who the heck was that, and why didn't I ignore their buddy request again?"

Mind Your Manners – LMAO – RT @CrAzY_gURL who knew you could roflcoptr appear less intelligent conversing in #onlineslang, or seem more incapable of getting a credible point across? While tempting to speak in common Internet parlance amongst fellow technorati (when in Rome et al… or at least on an Italian server), don't kid yourself. Though it may seem cool to other techies – and feel appropriate in certain company – to abandon the rules of grammar and punctuation, realize: To the rest of the English-speaking world, you just sound like a #nimrod.

Can the Spam – Uh-oh, don't tell social butterflies. If you don't actually know someone, psychologically, sending a direct message or writing on their wall is like leaning in for a kiss before you've even had your first date. Instead, try introducing yourself more gradually by interfacing with their status updates slowly at first – liking or retweeting them, leaving sporadic comments, etc. – to create a sense of familiarity before ramping up and going in for the kill. The ritual of online courtship may seem strange and terrifying at first, but as a rule, it's simple: As in real-life, it's best to try breaking the proverbial ice by chipping away at it instead of falling through kicking and screaming.

Chapter 9
WORKING WITH THE MEDIA:
CULTIVATE A WINNING PUBLIC IMAGE

In business, the eyes and ears of the world are constantly upon you – hence, you've always got to be on your "A" game. And as any seasoned PR specialist can tell you, how you present yourself is almost as, and in many cases more, important than the actual facts surrounding any situation. Chapter 8 talked about how to make headlines; this chapter will help you ensure that those headlines are positive. Understanding how to work with, and alongside, the press isn't just a key part of any business' ongoing responsibilities – at the end of the day, it's one of the core determinants used to ultimately influence public perception, and financial success by proxy.

The funny thing is, as discovered in a former decade-plus career as one of the world's most prolific business and technology journalists, many professional publicists still don't know how to successfully interface with the Fourth Estate. At best, it's a painful annoyance, creating major roadblocks that will prevent your business from ever being the focus of positive news stories, front-page mentions or widespread public recognition. At worst, it can cripple any chance you have at achieving fame and fortune, or send a former empire into a crumbling tailspin.

Happily, a seasoned and talented PR professional who knows how to work with editors can make a world of difference. It's a good thing too: Editors are known for their strong opinions, and aren't shy about expressing them. Learning how to better interface with the media isn't difficult. It just requires foreknowledge of a few simple guiding points.

Know Your Product

PR is nothing if not a glorified form of salesmanship. And as we're all aware, you can't effectively sell a product you don't know. Not only does it pay for PR reps to be informed about their product or service – it also pays to be genuinely enthusiastic about them.

Remember that passion, says Dean Bender, co-founder of Bender/Helper Impact, is what defines a successful PR rep from an ineffective one. Not only will this passion translate into being able to better think on your feet, respond to any questions the media might ask and achieve results with greater expediency. It also means you'll know exactly how to craft messaging, the best way to sell this message and when/where to place stories to achieve maximum coverage.

Plan Ahead

Opinions differ on how long it takes to plot out a proper PR campaign – some say a year, others six months or less. (Note: For certain products in crowded genres, e.g. apps, campaign cycles have tightened to as little as six to 12 weeks.) But one theme remains consistent across the board, as PR professionals know: You can't effectively promote a product or service without first having clearly-defined objectives and a master strategic plan in place. Essentially, to succeed with PR programs, you have to know exactly what type of product you're promoting, who the potential audience for it is, how to speak to them and what goals/expectations are realistic before ever making outreach.

Start by determining a product's release date. Then define its top selling points – the three to five features that make it unique from all of the other products out on the market. Come up with a way to get these messages across in 30 seconds or less, and within the first two sentences of any press release. Build a list of media outlets you'd like to connect with and decide on a dissemination strategy for each. Then create a tactical approach designed so that coverage breaks at carefully cultivated times, e.g. right before your sales team approaches retailers or so that print coverage arranged 90 days in advance coincides with the arrival of online stories. Whatever you do, try to coordinate it so it arrives in a tightly controlled window, to create the appearance of being everywhere at once. And for heaven's sake, make sure you have a steady supply of assets and chat-worthy tidbits designed to keep people talking throughout the entire period leading up to and on through the venture's launch.

Seize the Day

Director Woody Allen once said that "70% of success in life is showing up" – yours truly concurs. Just taking the time to recognize the value of public relations and making an attempt at outreach will put you way ahead of the pack. There's a reason many independent and small businesses fail to get decent media coverage – it's that they don't even try.

Even if you can't afford to throw fancy press junkets or have celebrity talent attached to your product, it's still possible to earn just as much coverage as those companies who do – doubly so with services like Help a Reporter Out (HARO) available. At the very least, merely shooting journalists (whatever their background) a simple email or giving them an occasional call on a regular basis when there's something new and noteworthy to discuss is crucial. Naturally, you don't want to be pushy or inundate anyone's inbox with spam. But the old maxim holds: "The squeaky wheel gets the grease." Staying top of mind is imperative.

At any time, for any reason, from an editorial standpoint, holes can suddenly open up in single pages or entire sections of magazines as advertisements and stories fall in and out… So when in doubt, never forget. You never know when opportunity will arise, and there's a chance for an unknown software program or small business to be featured alongside, and enjoy equal standing with, market leaders in a major media outlet.

Persistence pays, as does diligent follow-up. Just make sure when pitching you've taken the time to craft ideas for the specific outlet, know the right editor to speak to and where stories would fit within the publication. Can the blanket sales routine too: One size does NOT fit all. That goes double when dealing with consumer media – you'll get farther devising a timely, tangential hook to tie your product to. (Example: If there's a recession going on, tie it to a unique money-saving angle.) The proven trick to nailing a story every time: Finding an approach that helps products and services make sense not just as attractive narratives unto themselves, but also in an overall timely and cultural context for the outlet's specific readership.

Keep it Real

Successful public relations representatives know that much of the business is based entirely on relationships – practitioners with a proven track record and strong Rolodex get much further than those resigned to cold calls alone. Naturally, it's no secret that you should always cultivate a connection with the people you work with, especially members of the media, since, as in all walks of life, "you are who you know." But no matter how good the freebies you provide or flashy the parties you throw are, remember: Members of the press come to events to conduct outreach and do business, not slap hands and quaff free drinks. In other words, they're looking for substance, not pure flash and dazzle.

As former Funcom product director Jørgen Tharaldsen sagely put it once, it pays for PR reps to be honest, friendly, welcoming and knowledgeable – and truly mean what they say. So don't be the sort of shill who comes off so greasy you'd spontaneously combust if someone suddenly took a drag off a lit cigarette. Members of the press are trained to spot snake oil salesmen, and remember any shady overtures made, as well as sly, seemingly offhand remarks. Body language is important too: They'll notice if you're all smiles when shaking hands, but afterwards immediately turn away, attempt to escape conversation or become distracted when the next so-called big fish enters the room. It's OK to be awkward, or even apologetic, if you're new on the job and out of your depth. These are natural human responses people can empathize with. However you interface with the media though, it needs to be genuine.

Knowing this, it's vital to keep things on the level, act like a decent, respectful human being and always be on your best behavior around press, and actually care about them as people, not just tools to an end. PR professionals should also be willing to answer all questions with candor (or at least provide a clever enough response to not feel like you're dodging the question or steering back to the same message points over and over) and be reasonable when managing product expectations. Understand that you'll ultimately be judged by your actions and ability to deliver – not how fun you are to hang out with or how lavish an evening soiree you can throw.

Bear in mind as well that it's necessary to treat all members of the media equally – from broadcaster to blogger, it's a level playing field out there, and you can't afford to play favorites. You never know when the part-timer you've offended is destined to become the editor-in-chief of major influential consumer or trade site. Above all else, be supportive, even when there's nothing to be gained personally by doing so. And never, ever let friendships get in the way of business: The importance of maintaining a professional relationship, and the proverbial separation of church and state, can't be underrated.

You shouldn't take a scathing review or highly-critical editorial personal either. Everyone's entitled to their opinion – how would you react if you were told yours is wrong? And hey, you never know when a higher-up's stepped in and changed something, or a situation's otherwise out of an editor's control.

If you do have a problem with something someone's written, don't expect to change something that's already in print either. Call the writer and have a friendly, positive discussion explaining that you understand their point, clarify where you're coming from and ask for feedback so that things won't play out the same in the future. Never try to browbeat someone into taking a story back. The better solution: Suggest ways (say, the introduction of a new article that might cast your product or client in a better light) to meet in the middle, so everything evens out in the end.

Get the Job Done

Most importantly, if a journalist asks for something – a screenshot, an interview, a meeting with top execs, whatever – make sure you respond promptly, and do your best to deliver. They'll understand if the request falls through, so long as you've shown them enough respect to make the effort. Most members of the media are hard workers who'll do anything within ethical limits and the bounds of reason to make a story happen. As a sign of mutual appreciation and understanding, it's expected that you will too.

Always remember: Gaining an editor or freelancer's trust is easy, but it only takes one dropped ball to ruin your reputation with a journalist irrevocably. No story equals an unhappy writer, which equals wasted time, lost money and a teed-off bunch of folks all around. The upshot being that you've always got to be prepared to deliver assets, hands-on demonstrations, spokespeople or whatever else media need on-demand.

It sounds like common sense, but really… do your job to the best of your ability (be honest – you know when you're selling yourself, and others, short), and success will come. Ultimately, it's by being reliable that you'll install the highest level of confidence in your abilities and make yourself an indispensable resource amongst those you work with on both sides of the PR and media divide.

Paid Newswires: Valuable Resources or Out-of-Date?

In a world where small businesses can garner so much publicity for free though social and digital media outlets, is there really any benefit in using more traditional routes, such as paid newswires? The answer is both yes and no.

The goals of sending press releases over paid newswires such as **Vocus** and **PR Newswire** are manifold. Chief among them: Garnering publicity, raising brand awareness, introducing corporate leadership as a ready source of expertise, sourcing leads for potential business partnerships and, of course, generating interview opportunities and headlines. Many of these can be accomplished less formally through free social and digital media channels. However, by the same token, you shouldn't overlook paid newswire distribution as a crucial piece of any PR strategy. It all comes down to ROI. You must decide whether a paid newswire release is going to be "worth it" for your business.

As with marketing, generating positive PR is a function of building reach and frequency, and establishing yourself as a trusted source of information, helping to cultivate long-term relationships that ultimately pay off down the road. That said, one could justifiably make the argument that a single, well-connected PR representative or agency could prove just as, if not more, effective at raising awareness for your organization and its varied initiatives as any random media blast. Likewise, a number of free or discount wire services (e.g., **PRWeb**, **GamesPress**, **24-7 Press Release** or **PRLog**) reaching specific verticals can often provide greater efficacy at a fraction of the larger services' up-front cost. As such, it's imperative to always weigh potential costs and benefits and do the necessary research needed to comprehend how to best target a given audience.

"Worth It?": Measuring ROI

A common way to measure a campaign's ROI is by the volume of resulting online/print/video chatter, degree of headline/lead generation and the number of various requests for interviews or input that you receive. That said, not all paid releases land with as much of a splash as others do. It helps to set realistic expectations going in (face it: not every story's front page news), and to have a clear idea of the overall story your enterprise or brand is attempting to tell.

Not all results are immediately quantifiable either. Many times, you'll make successful outreach only to find out later that the reason the message ultimately got through is because you'd been able to generate some degree of trust and familiarity with the brand name as a result of the individual or group having come across a previous release or two in passing. Results are often hard to measure in terms of hard numbers, which – at least from an executive budgeting standpoint – can make paid press release distribution a tough sell.

But what paid newswires can do is aid in reach, by putting you in front of a wider media audience, and assist with search engine optimization, because many can garner guaranteed space on high-ranking sites like Yahoo! Choose appropriate keywords ("online shopping cart," "mobile payments," "accounting software," etc.) and link back to sites you're trying to move up the search results rankings, and you may be able to glean benefits, regardless of actual editorial coverage. Whether it's worth $99-$500+ to accomplish these tasks is a question you'll have to ask yourself, however, and depends entirely on campaign objectives.

For the record, we typically advise reserving paid release distribution for only the largest announcements. Similarly, it's also best to choose those solutions with the most guaranteed reach on major media sites, as the more incoming links from higher-ranking and more established outlets your websites enjoy, the better their search engine optimization (SEO). Note that as we've learned from experience, you'll often garner more publicity from direct contact and follow-up with individual journalists. (A point which applies to any form of press release, whether you distribute through a direct mailing list or newswire – circling back on pitches is mandatory.) Still, if you set aside share of voice – dedicated newswire sections, even on major media outlets, aren't exactly prime real estate ripe for generating clicks – and focus on long-term gains, newswires can prove useful, actual story-generating performance notwithstanding.

Providing a potential chance to boost your ranking in search results for perennially popular terms (insurance company, document storage, law firm Los Angeles, identity theft expert, etc.), they may pay dividends over an extended horizon. Knowing this, you may find that they ultimately justify the cost, and allow you to amortize it over many potential contacts and stories to come. Those focused on immediate results, however, may struggle to justify the investment.

Paid Newswires as a Piece of the PR Puzzle

Always remember, though: Release distribution through paid newswires is only one element of any well-orchestrated public relations plan. Just as vital is actual face-to-face time and relationship-building with members of the media, conducting successful follow-up and making ongoing outreach through both traditional and social networking channels.

Paid newswire distribution can certainly augment any PR strategy, helping announcements reach a targeted audience of highly-influential journalists and tastemakers, as well as circulate across industry-leading websites. But it shouldn't be the sole tentpole upon which you hang your organization's plan of attack. Given the sheer volume of information that today's industry professionals are bombarded with from second-to-second, it's all too simple for a single missive, no matter how ostensibly important, to get swallowed up in a sea of white noise.

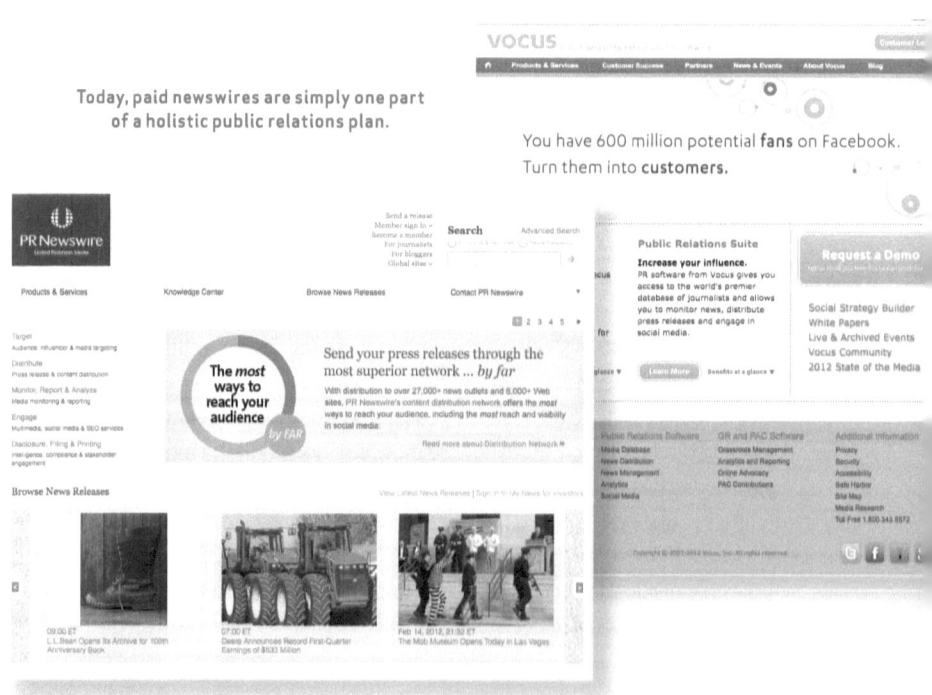

Today, paid newswires are simply one part of a holistic public relations plan.

Chapter 10
USING TWITTER TO BOOST YOUR BUSINESS

Between billboards, TV spots and event-based advertising, corporate giants like Coca-Cola, Rogers and Shell often boast marketing budgets comparable to third-world nations' GDPs. So how's a small-business owner to compete?

The answer is simple: In 140 characters or less.

Whereas Chapter 4 talked about general online marketing strategies, this chapter focuses on one particular resource that can boost your business by leaps and bounds: Popular micro-blogging service Twitter. Ashton Kutcher, Shaquille O'Neal and, yes, even Oprah swear by it. (Although Kutcher's ill-advised comments, which at one point caused him to hand over his account to his marketing firm, Katalyst Media, for management, may have prompted second thoughts.) But here's a dirty secret you might not know about Twitter, which lets users enter and share 140-character-or-less text messages and online links (a.k.a. "tweets"): With 175 million users who send over 200 million real-time updates a day, it's a classic case study in frequency and reach. Readily transportable between connected online devices from smartphones to tablets and PCs, tweets not only travel wherever users do, but they also constantly keep certain topics, individuals and, naturally, businesses top of mind. Twitter can help you affordably promote your business and provide significant cost savings.

The platform's most obvious use: Creating an online following for corporate leaders, brands or enterprises. (Come visit yours truly at @GadgetExpert – it's always a pleasure to connect.) Thank the social fabric of the service, whereby users essentially register to "follow," or receive ongoing updates from, specific individuals – and frequently "retweet," or re-post and pass featured missives along. As such, it's possible to quickly become a trusted source for information on, or expert in, any given subject. And, naturally, amass a dedicated audience of fans who willingly desire to regularly engage in dialogue concerning (and learn more about) a given topic or brand. To wit, it's not unusual to see everyday users or at-home businesses with thousands or even tens of thousands of followers. All of which, naturally, adds up to a dedicated fan base you can source new ideas and market research from, or appeal directly to with any new product or service.

However, given Twitter's sheer ability to fuel word-of-mouth buzz and viral pickup, savvy entrepreneurs are also exploiting its potential to directly drive additional sales and generate heightened in-store traffic. Thanks to an explosion in popularity, given widespread media attention from outlets like *The New York Times* and CBS, even your friendly neighborhood hamburger joint and ice cream stand are hopping onboard, posting regular specials and updates. Credit the service's hyper-local focus, which allows community members to easily sync up and share information. As such, even the smallest mom and pop stand can suddenly compete with larger-scale concerns, and, for that matter, connect for free with a customer base previously reachable only via limited hand-to-hand pass-along, direct contact/mailings, weekly circulars or ads in the local paper.

Just ask businesses like Umi Sushi (@umi), who are leveraging the power of the platform to reach thousands of potential customers. "In an economy like this, small business owners need to spread the word efficiently and affordably," explains Steve Strauss (@SteveStrauss), author of *The Small Business Bible*. "Social networking is word of-mouth advertising for the 21st century… and that's the best advertising there is."

The kicker is that such communications can also be more effective, since information sharing now works in real-time and travels both ways. (A major plus if you're attempting to monitor active chatter concerning your brand – or put out a major publicity fire.) Customers can literally speak up and provide instant feedback on the latest flavor of gelato, see what's on today's lunch menu or even provide suggestions for tomorrow's blue plate special.

Business owners are additionally taking advantage of the service's instant gratification mentality to post timed discounts ("act now to save 25%," "free shipping for the first five customers," etc.), cash-saving coupon codes and noteworthy deals or bargains. Ironically, the more frequently you point shoppers towards the juiciest savings, or re-post those that others have found, the more attention and eyeballs you'll attract. Even giants like Walgreens (@Walgreens) and Marriott (@MarriottIntl) are getting in on the game, actively interfacing with the public to build trust and offering one-of-a-kind bargains that help keep these brands top of mind and inspire customer loyalty. Building consumer confidence requires more than just registering for the service and tossing out the odd sound byte, though, with consistency and quality of updates vital to success. In what can only be seen as a win-win for both consumers and small businesses, it creates an environment wherein it's essential to forge lasting relationships, and provide a greater degree of open dialogue and transparency between both parties.

No surprise then that industry leaders like WalMart (@WalmartSpecials), Delta (@Delta) and Starbucks (@Starbucks) all use Twitter to drive direct sales, offer promotional discounts and engage shoppers with their brand. But from small specialty restaurants (@DaLeveeCajun) to mentoring services (@boldlybeautiful) and real estate brokers (@RealLivingHER), a legion of scrappy upstarts are also using it to turbo-charge their business.

"Twitter's been great for business," says Doug Burgoyne, founder of Vancouver-based FROGBOX (@FROGBOX), a provider of sustainable alternatives to cardboard moving boxes. "It's always one of the top five referral sources to our website." Burgoyne, who uses the service to communicate with customers and promote environmental awareness, says it's prompted a 5X increase in online traffic and increased his company's sales by 18%.

"Twitter has become an amazing tool to promote sales, blog posts, reviews and [product] giveaways," agrees Tamiko Hargrove, CEO of New York-based scented candle maker Helen Julia (@helenjuliainc). Hargrove, who uses the service to raise awareness for special bargains and contests, says it continues to bring in 8-10 new customers monthly, and prompted a whopping 50% increase in website traffic. New Orleans based NakedPizza (@NakedPizza) has also been pleasantly surprised with Twitter's impact, as tweeting weekly specials, online-only discounts and links to its electronic newsletter and blog now accounts for 15%-60% of ongoing sales depending on the week and promotion. Likewise, Salt Lake City, Utah custom shoemaker Kuru Footwear (@kuru_footwear) can additionally vouch for the service's effectiveness, crediting its social media efforts with causing January 2010 revenues to more than double initial projections.

Toronto-based Snakehead Games (@starpiratesgame), creator of online amusement Star Pirates, has also been thrilled with Twitter's impact. The firm not only found that buying paid tweets from celebrities – one of many popular options for marketing on the service – generated up to 700% more click-throughs than traditional Internet advertisements and resulted in over 1000 new account signups. It further discovered that the service was a great way to generate awareness and build support from fans. "The real value of Twitter is as a two-way communication tool that allows you to build a community amongst people who have similar interests," says Snakehead director Colin Ferguson. "It shows that we're responsive to users' opinions, which directly or indirectly turns into sales."

Tom Drake, a personal finance guru who self-publishes the Canadian Finance Blog (@CanadianFinance), is also a believer. "In March of 2009, [we had] 816 visits," he says. "One year after starting to use Twitter to promote the site, we now receive almost 30,000 visits a month, and [have earned] near $4000 in advertising sales. It's allowed my wife to stay home and care for our baby beyond the maternity leave period."

"Twitter is powerful, free and ubiquitous," confirms Guy Kawasaki (@guykawasaki), co-founder of Alltop.com and a noted social media personality with over 465,000 followers on Twitter himself. "It's hard to beat that as a combination for small business marketing."

As for other potential benefits Twitter offers beyond helping entrepreneurs draw attention to clever sales promotions ("All scarves half off tomorrow"), exclusive giveaways ("Free hot dogs for the next five customers to tweet us back!") and advertising efforts ("Come experience our state-of-the-art, eco-friendly furniture showroom")? Consider the ability to search for trending topics and keywords (e.g., product names), letting you quickly gauge public interest in your wares or connect with potential business partners and nearby customers shopping for services in your area. Alternately, as in the case of Los Angeles street taco vendor Kogi BBQ (@KogiBBQ), who regularly publicizes its trucks' arrival at upcoming locations via Twitter only to find hundreds of people waiting, it's also a great way to raise overall brand awareness. A great way to source instant feedback, Twitter is even being used by 75-year-old companies like Cromer's P-Nuts (@cromerspnuts), who are finding the service an innovative, cost-effective way to gauge shopper excitement and conduct informal focus group testing.

But above all else, most small biz owners say there's no better tool for facilitating enhanced customer service. "We actually had a Twitter user (@clayco) come in who wasn't impressed with whatever he ordered and tweeted about it," confesses Umi co-owner Russell Richardson. "But another Twitter user went back-and-forth with him and convinced him that he'd ordered improperly. Now, @clayco is a regular guest at our restaurant and absolutely loves everything – if it wasn't for Twitter, he might not have been convinced."

"What's really demonstrated the power of Twitter to us is the relative ease of accessibility [it offers for keeping in contact with customers]," concurs Kuru's social networking consultant Nathan Mathews. "It's easier for people to respond via short tweets rather than having to draft email responses or arrange talk times via phone."

How to build a following, though? Easy, claim experts like Kawasaki – just be clever, outgoing and heavy on the chutzpah.

"There are three main ways for small businesses [to get the word out]," agrees Strauss. The first step, he advises: Just be social, join in the conversation, and use the service to network and meet new people. ("That's how many people [generate] new business with Twitter," he says, "through the new relationships they create.") Second, make a point of re-tweeting, or forwarding, news on must-see specials, sales and updates, which won't just attract a loyal following, but also prompt recipients to pass the word, and your contact info, along. Last, but not least, he says, focus on tweeting valuable information – not just idle chatter or self-serving drivel. "Get known as an expert," he advises. "Give, and people will follow you and you will build your brand."

There are a few common mistakes to avoid along the way, however. For starters, don't hide your contact info – website URLs and email addresses are a must-have for customers who can't say all they need within Twitter's space limitations. Also make a point of responding to all queries in a timely fashion: As a highly personal means of communication, customers expect a prompt answer, just as they would if they called your office. Going easy on hard sales pitches is additionally advised, with a more conversational approach – and an indirect one at that – to marketing preferable for the Twitter audience. As a rule of thumb, it's vital to deliver on promises as well, as transparency is crucial when working with social media. Skip the hyperbole wherever possible. Consistency is critical too. Out of sight, out of mind, or so they say… a fact that goes double with fickle online audiences.

Granted, there's no one surefire strategy for success. What you take away from the service also depends on what you put into it. Nor, say insiders, is return on investment always easily quantifiable, citing the added danger of spending so much time experimenting with the service that you overlook other, more potentially lucrative business opportunities.

Still, as it requires no actual up-front cash outlay or risk beyond one's time investment, across the board, experts agree that Twitter should be an essential part of any modern small business' social media strategy.

"It's the cheapest, fastest and potentially most useful social media advertising tool," says Kawasaki. "While no one really knows what marketing approaches will work here for sure, what is there to lose by trying? It's completely free."

Top Twitter Apps and Services

■ **TweetMeme** – Adds a "retweet" button to any story on your blog or website, allowing users to share it. Note that the more tweets it has, the more value the article is perceived to contain from viewers' perspective, potentially generating massive reader pass-along.

■ **Twitterfeed** – Publishes your latest blog posts or RSS feed to Twitter and Facebook, allowing you to ensure that all your social media is integrated.

■ **HootSuite** – Lets you schedule tweets to go live at set times, monitor chatter surrounding your brand, balance workflow between a team of contributors and track clicks and customer engagement.

■ **CoTweet** – Offers an enterprise-level solution for businesses looking to manage multiple Twitter accounts, track rising keywords and trends and delegate the duty of responding to incoming messages between numerous individuals.

■ **TweetDeck** – Lets you juggle multiple accounts, filter and track information of relevance and keep abreast of breaking news of interest via notification alerts.

Save Money with Twitter

Clearly, as you can see from successful small business owners' and industry experts' feedback, Twitter doesn't have to be just another mindless distraction keeping you from focusing on growing and maintaining your small business. Instead, it can be a vehicle that helps significantly boost brand awareness, provides for cost-effective marketing and, most importantly, brings smiling customers sprinting through your doors. But what many entrepreneurs may not realize is that you can also use it to save on everything from equipment to ongoing overhead, and shave precious dollars off your monthly burn rate. Here are three tips for saving money with Twitter.

1 **Hunt for Deals by Keyword** – Business owners can use Twitter to realize immediate, tangible savings on new office equipment, gadgets and technology. To instantly trim expenditures, start by using the search function and seeking out fiscally-minded terms such as "coupon," "deal," "bargain," "discount," "coupon code," "on sale," "10% off," or "free shipping." After sifting through results to determine which are most relevant, you'll also get a sense of which fellow users do the best job of consistently reporting on steals in the categories you most favor. Follow them, and you'll be able to use the power of crowdsourcing to receive a running, and ever-growing, feed of the deals likeliest to suit your needs. If time's hard to come by, bargain aggregators like **CouponTweet.com** and **CheapTweet.com** can also sift through all the white noise and quickly point you towards the hottest discounts.

2 **Register for Sales and Specials** – Be sure to sign up to receive updates from companies like Dell, WalMart and JetBlue as well, who all use the service to promote value-minded specials. Similarly, popular cash-saving online communities such as Fat Wallet (@fatwalletdeals), BensBargains (@bensbargains), SlickDeals (@slickdeals) and RetailMeNot (@retailmenot) maintain running feeds too. If your schedule permits, it additionally pays to track down local user groups and publications native to your city, as they often have a better handle on bargains happening just a block away. Also be sure to follow pennywise publications including Entrepreneur (@EntMagazine), CNN Money (@CNNMoney) and Inc. Magazine (@IncMagazine), who know how vital savings can be. Most importantly, don't hesitate to pass along word of any deals you find for others to access, which helps add to your fan base, grow credibility and build positive karma.

3 **Join the Online Social** – Look for local publications and communities that issue deal updates through Twitter to find steals and deals specific to your industry, hometown or geographic area. After all, you never know when a freebie is literally waiting right around the next corner, or potential vendor is offering a steal on a product of interest. Also be sure to tweet or retweet any deals you find, which will help make you a trusted source for this information, thereby prompting people to follow you and increasing the chances followers will pass along deals of their own, ensuring the cash-saving cycle continues…

Take advantage of the multitude of savings to be found through
companies and apps that use Twitter to communicate deals.

Chapter 11
BUILDING AN ONLINE COMMUNITY: 10 TIPS FOR SUCCESS

All companies, no matter their size, rely on the support and goodwill of customers to survive in today's market – doubly so in an online world, where hundreds of competitors are literally just a click away. But the harsh reality is that some are better than others at learning to engage and interact with these individuals, all of whom share a very important common interest: Your small business.

Those who fall into the former camp enjoy some crucial benefits – e.g. better CRM, heightened loyalty, greater insight into their target market, improved sales, enhanced shopper feedback, etc. Those who don't constantly watch opportunity fly out the window. As such, the importance of cultivating one's community can't be understated, especially given that the costs of acquiring new customers can often outstrip those of selling to existing clients by tenfold.

Looking for a few simple, cost-effective and inventive ways to spark your audience's interest? Here are some tips for building a vocal and passionate online community that anyone can feel proud to be a part of.

1 Provide an Open Forum for Discussion – The first rule of community engagement: Establish a dedicated, persistent venue where users can feel comfortable sharing, discussing and debating whatever's top of mind. Note that this outlet can take the form of a message board, newsgroup, online forum, custom social network or even Facebook fan page. A company blog can also make a compelling vehicle for ongoing conversation, allowing you to source users' opinions and engage them in active dialogue. However, whichever solution you ultimately choose, it's essential that you make a commitment to regularly updating and maintaining it. Part of this promise needs to include providing ongoing responses to users' queries and nurturing new and existing lines of discussion.

2 Connect and Communicate – Make no bones about it: Blogging should be an essential part of any modern website. After all, a few clicks is literally all it takes to post updates in real-time around the clock, creating a steady stream of content that promises something new and exciting with every visit. Better still, professionals at all experience levels have the capability of readily doing it, and the practice also helps put a personal face on your organization, shining the spotlight on the individuals behind it. However, to really captivate an audience enough to keep them returning, take note: You'll also need to provide content that's dynamic, unique and offers measurable informational or entertainment value, plus speak in a language that all can understand. In short, the occasional pre-approved sound bite from the HR guy or gal won't cut it. Rather, you need to address audiences like you're having a normal conversation, and provide content with meaningful substance to the reader. Making-of articles, features detailing how to get more from your products, partner profiles, project diaries, step-by-step how-to guides, interviews with notable personalities or internal stakeholders: All present compelling ways to connect with audiences while also keeping them interested and informed, providing ample incentive to keep coming back.

3 **Employ Social Media Elements** – Designed to help users connect and spread the word, these platforms and services allow word-of-mouth buzz to spring up like wildfire. By giving audience members the power to re-tweet stories amongst themselves, share links to items and happenings of note via Facebook or Google+, and embed interesting pieces of content on their own websites, you do two things. You not only expand your reach far beyond an initial distribution list, all while providing links back to the original source, which allow new individuals with similar interests to discover and become a part of the movement. (Not to mention aid with search engine optimization.) You also create a sense of momentum behind any update and allow it to potentially snowball in excitement.

4 **Emphasize Community Building** – As social media insiders well know, creating a sense of community around your website is one of the most powerful tools for engaging and ultimately enthralling prospective fans. But doing so doesn't simply mean throwing up a sponsored message board and then leaving it to stagnate or emailing customers sporadic newsletter updates that regurgitate existing material easily found elsewhere. Rather, you have to not only encourage discussion and actively take part in conversations by dedicating internal time and resources, but you also need to make customers feel as if they truly have a voice in the discussion by listening to their concerns, responding and sourcing feedback at every opportunity. Implementing programs that recognize and reward valued contributors is also vital, as is creating fan-based initiatives that allow community members to contribute and share ideas, concepts and creations of their own. Even simple gestures like giving enthusiasts the chance to submit designs for your next fundraiser's logo or arranging times where they can chat with top execs to provide input on upcoming ventures won't just engender goodwill. They'll also excite and empower a legion of amateur brand ambassadors – an essential source of free ongoing updates and constructive conversations which will both attract users to and keep them enamored with your site.

5 **Design for Mass Distribution** – Sharing is good – even more so if you've got a message worth spreading and it winds up in front of millions of eyeballs. As such, you should be not only updating your website with unique pieces of content (surveys, research reports, custom editorial clips, guides to solving common problems, unique looks behind-the-scenes, etc.) designed to grab viewers' attention, but you should also make everything from blog posts to pictures, infographics, PDF documents and videos shareable, embeddable and ready to be commented upon or re-tweeted via social media platforms. When it comes to corporate assets, the tendency – especially amongst hyper-competitive start-ups – is always to tightly hold and control. But often, the more powerful strategy is to design pieces of content with the specific idea in mind of seeding them throughout the user community, as it's a great way to build brand awareness. Beyond heightened exposure and additional media mentions, using your website to disseminate unique, specially-branded pieces of content can also lead to improved search engine optimization results through a larger number of incoming links. And, more importantly still, these pieces of content generate heightened word of mouth surrounding your homepage, letting countless potential readers know exciting things are happening there on a regular basis.

6 **Make a Lasting Commitment** – The joy of online and social media services is that these platforms make the entire world feel close at-hand. As such, people enjoy a greater sense of one-to-one connection while using them, and expect you and your business to be both present and listening. So before setting up that Twitter account, Google Plus profile or Facebook fan page, consider: You'll be expected to make regular updates, actually respond to users' comments and not disappear for days on end while reams of canned responses or ghostwritten clips serve as filler. Certainly, a busy executive can't be expected to be checking their accounts personally every minute of every day. But whether you hire dedicated community managers to help or simply split up social media duties amongst existing team members, someone's always got to man the front lines.

7 **Focus on Value** – Exclusive specials, contests, promotions and timed discounts can all be powerful drivers of website traffic, especially in these cost-conscious times. By offering direct bargains and rebate programs on both an ongoing and sporadic basis through your online headquarters, you can keep customers' interest piqued, and generate additional sales. These marketing programs become even more valuable when coupled with Facebook, Twitter and other social marketing tools which have the potential to help news spread like wildfire online. Just make sure that the only place such bargains can be found is on your homepage, and be consistent in the page(s) to where you drive this traffic, to establish in shoppers' minds the importance of regularly checking a certain online destination. Similarly, establishing relationships with key influencers, bloggers and members of the media can also help get the word out, as can a regular series of email or newsletter updates designed to inform current and prospective buyers. Customers get to save on purchases while you benefit from enhanced publicity and heightened sales, creating a win-win situation for all.

8 **Use Targeted Demonstrations** – While special membership options, premium subscription packages and frequent buyer programs can all prove great incentives, oftentimes, services that you freely give away are just as important as those which you reserve for more exclusive clients. Whether you're looking at offering complimentary computer virus scans by having users visit your homepage, providing a suite of free continuing education resources or simply hosting an archive of complementary, corporate-branded webinars on software engineering, realize. Providing helpful services or information at no charge that solve pressing, evergreen problems or answer important questions can all serve to generate a steady source of online traffic, and provide a ready supply of leads to upsell on premium services. Translation: Sometimes you have to give in order to get. It may seem counterintuitive. But ultimately, the practice makes a ready way to demonstrate your organization's capabilities to a potentially lucrative client base, while also giving them a taste of the benefits to be had by partnering on more advanced or long-term services.

9 Empower End-Users – No matter how many resources you throw at a project, there's no competing with the sheer creativity, imagination and raw output of the public at large. Moreover, unconstrained by issues like budgets, deadlines and corporate politics, users are often able to produce works of sheer genius that would otherwise be difficult for entrepreneurial outfits and large-scale enterprises alike. Therefore, it often pays to let community members themselves take an active role producing and policing content. Wise business owners will also recognize and reward top performers (with special status and titles, virtual badges, access to exclusive events, free product, etc.) for their contributions, which make online communities more effective and compelling for all involved.

10 Tap the Power of Crowdsourcing – Ultimately, people take part in communities to engage and interact with others within the context of each group's unique social fabric. Giving them the ability to participate in the design and construction of various supporting elements doesn't only allow them to do just that. (Say, by allowing users to submit designs for your new site's logo or layout, then vote the best to the top, or create custom posters starring your company's mascot for email sharing with friends and family.) It also provides an opportunity for them to be recognized for their work, and have a lasting impact on both the community at large and the product, service or subject it's based around. These practices can quickly generate empathy and enthusiasm, and – as a crucial added benefit – reinforce that you value your community members and their contributions.

Mind you, while no single strategy will work for every online community, as each consists of its own distinct collective of individuals and perspectives, the good news is as follows: With the right mix of insight and enthusiasm, not to mention the multitude of free online tools available to small business owners, any entrepreneur can potentially galvanize thousands of fans and supporters into action. Knowing this, you don't have to be a publicist, politician or even reality TV star to set the Internet ablaze, and enjoy the thrill of knowing you've rallied countless customers to your cause.

Chapter 12
INDIVIDUAL PR:
PROMOTING A SELF-PUBLISHED BOOK

Producing an eBook or print on-demand manuscript can be a fantastic way to establish yourself as a subject matter expert and create brand awareness. Doing so is also easier than ever and, thanks to the rise of mobile devices, can help you touch more individuals and generate a higher number of impressions in a shorter period of time than ever before. (See Chapter 2 for tools and services that make doing so quick and simple.) Daunting as the prospect of actually writing the volume seems – and make no mistake, it's still a time-consuming, albeit enjoyable, process – don't be fooled: Managing the volume's promotion is just as challenging and important.

Dozens of freelance copywriters and ghostwriting or graphic design services promise to help authors capitalize on the power of digital distribution to grow their business and gain attention from online, print and TV journalists. But what they don't tell would-be authors is that upwards of 10,000 publishers join the fray every year, and roughly nine out of every 10 books sell less than 1000 copies. In fact, many veteran authors jokingly refer to these books as "business cards," as what they really do is establish expertise, providing a platform through which to gain media attention, or start lucrative speaking or training practices. Regardless of why you choose to write, whether for personal or professional reasons, to achieve any degree of success with the volume – outside, of course, of the sense of accomplishment you rightly deserve – be aware: You'll need to get it in front of as many people as possible. That means having to publicize it.

Given that your budget for promotions is likely far smaller than those of large publishing houses, how do you make sure your advertising and PR efforts reach and influence the right people? Consider capitalizing on eight tips that can help you stand out and promote more efficiently and effectively.

1 Look the part – You may have heard the expression "fake it till you make it," typically used in unflattering terms. But what those who utter the phrase with disdain don't realize is that it refers to the vital art of learning to punch above your weight. In other words, how you package and present yourself is crucial in a world where first impressions are hugely important.

To this extent, start by creating an official company name under which to publish your manuscript, build a professional-looking website (hint: premade templates can help) and ask a pal in PR to handle media inquiries as a favor. All it takes is five minutes to set up natty-looking corporate email addresses as well, even if they're just info@ or press@yourbook.com – it sounds much sharper than SomeChump@gmail.com. Likewise, companies like **eVoice** can help you set up toll-free numbers with professionally-recorded greetings and extensions (even though "dial three for accounting" forwards to your cat) for pennies on the dollar.

The bottom line: Look like a professional outfit, and that's how you'll be perceived. Take the time to craft a winning image, and casual observers won't stop to wonder if your operation is staffed by one or 50, or worry about increasingly outdated vanity press stereotypes.

2 **Source advance quotes to build credibility** – Need to cement your expertise, or worried about being subject to public criticism? You can instantly garner street cred and accolades by asking recognized experts (authors, journalists, thought leaders, leading execs, etc.) in your field to provide endorsement quotes for the manuscript before even announcing it. ("A must-read." – Malcolm Gladwell, Author, *The Tipping Point*.)

Such comments lend credibility to the volume, establish its value in the eyes of observers and can help you build buzz for a book before anyone even bothers to read a single page. Most individuals whose quotes are featured like the recognition boost and media attention such appearances bring as well, and may provide a ready excuse for them to help cross-promote the volume, e.g. through social media mentions. So don't be afraid to aim high when making outreach – you never know who'll be game to put in a good word.

3 **Reach out to the press and public** – Need a quick way to get the ball rolling? Grab a press list from a friendly PR representative and issue a series of media releases – product launch, ship date, notable discounts, etc. Then follow up by directly reaching out to the editors you feel will be most receptive with a genuine, personal note. Yes, you'll feel like an annoying jerk, but given the amount of distractions we all have to sift through these days, it's no wonder that when it comes to public awareness, the loudest voices are the ones most heard. If you believe in your book and feel there's a good fit, there's no shame in doing your best to bring it to people's attention.

Don't be afraid to reach out to other authors and websites or blogs that cover similar topics too, whether to provide a bylined article, offer books for contests and giveaways, or simply engage in discussion. Grassroots movements take time to cultivate, and there's no better source of support than an existing community.

4 **Be singular and original** – Any time you pitch your book or manuscript, message it from an original angle, and preferably tie its subject matter to a topical hook. Any trends or newsworthy events currently making headlines provide an opportune place to start (ex: if a celebrity's gotten into trouble for inappropriate texts, maybe now's the time to suggest a guide to high-tech etiquette). Similarly, make sure you position your book, where appropriate, as the first to explore a certain topic/theory or approach a subject from a unique slant.

The more you can tie the volume to something that's already caught people's eye and won't be going away soon (i.e. cost-consciousness, the green craze, extreme couponing, etc.), or give it a one-of-a-kind spin, the better. You'll get much further promoting a book on a subject the public's attention is already focused on than trying to convince already overworked reporters there's a story somewhere else that requires additional digging and footwork.

5 Make sure time is on your side – Whatever angle you choose to work, it helps for it to be resurgent from time to time in terms of public awareness, so you can ride these waves of interest as they ebb and flow over an extended horizon. If not, you run the risk of losing relevancy.

As evidenced by *The New York Times* bestseller charts, and continued success of volumes like Walter Isaacson's *Steve Jobs*, time-sensitive releases can often do very well when buoyed by emerging trends or recent events. But personally-produced projects are often slow to boil and can take years to make an impact. For self-published volumes, it helps to make sure you don't grow stale in the interim by finding ways to stay top of mind. Note: This may require reworking your book's message slightly to reflect the spirit of the times - e.g. yesterday's expert on personal finance and money-saving strategies is today's "recessionista."

Whenever possible, to maximize ROI, we always recommend focusing manuscripts on evergreen topics.

6 Two words: First or best – From both a positioning and project standpoint, you should always be the only or absolute top source of information on a given subject. All messaging, from the website to book jacket to volume itself to interviews you give, should also reflect and reinforce this topic and associated keywords. Given the pace of life these days, people tend to go off first impressions, and stick with the most widely-recognized (and thus easiest to remember and reference) sources. Therefore, it's best to keep it simple – and super compelling – for today's time- and attention-starved audiences.

7 Don't be afraid to ask for a favor – If you're an existing journalist or frequent media commentator who's expanding into the world of book authorship, you may enjoy a head start when it comes to promoting manuscripts. Most members of the press won't mind giving you a nod and promoting the project, as long as you're OK with them mentioning in the write-up that you're a contributor or making a joke about "of course he's an authority, he works for us."

But don't go in with a sense of entitlement: Expecting members of the media to show favoritism isn't just misguided, it's also unethical. Still, as in any field, there's no substitute for having established relationships you can reach out to. Journalists are always on the hunt for credible, trusted sources – swamped as many are, it helps if you're already on their list of contacts.

Don't have any friends in the Fourth Estate? As referenced earlier, Help a Reporter Out (<u>HARO</u>) can help you make some.

8 Know where you're headed – It's been suggested that as many as 94% of all books sell 999 or fewer copies, with most racking up entire tens of sales, so don't write a book for the money. Instead, look at it as a platform to establish your credentials, and get whatever message you feel matters across.

Publish a book – even via self-publishing methods – and you're suddenly an expert in its given subject. So figure out what you're after: Is it a chance to give something back to the community? Do you simply want to raise awareness about a specific topic? Is it a potential launchpad to a new career? Then figure out who the most receptive audience will be, and find a way to put both yourself and the volume in front of them.

This may involve giving away free copies to industry notables (hint: this is most affordable and efficiently done as a digital manuscript), handing books out at conferences, or partnering with organizations to include copies in gift bags, and come at personal expense. But know the path before you set out on it, and you'll know where and how to best work the manuscript. Succeed or fail, look on the bright side: Even the most niche or nondescript volume is good for the occasional speaking opportunity, which can potentially lead to more business or even a lucrative contract with a professional publishing house. Everyone – including tomorrow's bestselling author – has to get their start somewhere.

Self-publishing electronically or printing a physical book helps you establish credibility in your field of expertise.

PART 3

TECHNOLOGY
IT AND MOBILE SOLUTIONS

Chapter 13
RECENT TECHNOLOGY TRENDS:
LEADING THE WAY IN BUSINESS DEVICES

From smartphones to tablet PCs, GPS navigation systems to eReaders, technology is suddenly everywhere. Credit professionals' growing need for mobility and access to real-time information, helping fuel increasing demand for portable devices and spur the ubiquitous growth of apps, online services and social networks.

But whereas everyday shoppers are rallying behind high-tech phenomena such as connected TVs, streaming multimedia receivers and location-based savings and services, trends in business gadgets and technologies are charting a somewhat divergent course. For the coming years, focus will instead lie on more intuitive and powerful portable productivity solutions, tools which facilitate greater virtualization and accessories that make everyday tasks and mobile communications simpler. That many also incorporate features popular with the general public at large, e.g. casual videoconferencing, breezy wireless connectivity and social media or crowdsourced content is just an added bonus.

Following are five trends that promise to define the coming years' best business gadgets, each all but inevitably destined to filter their way into any enterprise over the coming months.

4G – Wireless cellular carriers such as AT&T, Verizon, Sprint and T-Mobile are all embracing the high-speed 4G Internet bandwagon and 4G LTE networks. Expect each to trot out a growing variety of handsets which utilize turbo-charged networks that allow small business owners to enjoy Web surfing and downloads at minimum speeds roughly 3-4X faster than current 3G standards. From the Droid Charge, capable of acting as a mobile hotspot for up to 10 WiFi devices, to the Samsung Galaxy S2, which adds an attractive, oversized 4.3" Super AMOLED plus display, choices will be multitudinous. Regardless of whether or not you need a brawny, dual-core processor-powered model like the Motorola Atrix 2 (capable of docking with a full-size screen to double as a laptop), expect marked speed boosts across the board. Not only should such advancements aid modern executives, who are accessing more online information and multimedia than ever, but also provide a ready platform for impromptu videoconferencing from a number of handsets.

Tablet PCs Take Over – With hundreds of tablets having flooded the market or been announced for release in recent months, and Google's uber-popular Android operating system increasingly being optimized for use with such units, it's becoming painfully obvious. Following upon the iPad's unprecedented success, manufacturers are convinced that these touchscreen units, more portable and intuitive than standard laptops, are the future of mobile computing. Name any consumer electronics giant from Asus to Lenovo, Sharp to Sony, and they've got models coming, with notables like the Asus Eee Pad Transformer Prime, Samsung's Galaxy Tab, and Motorola's Xoom just the tip of the iceberg. And of course, Apple's iPad has already taken the world by storm, with dual cameras for FaceTime video calling, slimmer styling and the power to juggle thousands of feature-adding apps. While business uses for such devices have been primarily confined to presentations, Web surfing or graphic design functions in the past, things are rapidly changing as we speak. Given new offerings from Microsoft, HP, Toshiba and more, and an ever-widening range of dedicated business and cloud computing apps, you can likewise count on much wider support for these platforms from productivity software makers going forward.

Apps Everywhere – Call them apps, widgets or good old-fashioned software programs. From Apple's Mac App Store and Intel's ultrabook-focused AppUp digital distribution channel to a widening range of TVs by LG, Samsung, Sony and Vizio with full Internet connectivity and support for downloadable apps, expect to find them everywhere going forward. Easy to browse, sample and enjoy virtually anytime, anywhere from a burgeoning range of devices (ranging from notebook PCs to eReaders, Bluetooth headsets and even cars by Ford, BMW and Toyota), consider it a welcome development. Using these bite-sized, value-priced applications, you can instantly transform your smartphone into a portable translator, invoicing system or inventory management platform, or research a prospective client and make lunch reservations while cruising to work. Although it's easy to become overwhelmed by the countless entrepreneur-friendly options currently being offered for download, e.g. database management tool **FileMaker Go** and customized brand-building solutions like **Mobile Roadie**, upsides are plentiful. Think streamlined controls, budget pricing, on-demand accessibility and, of course, the ability to add an effectively infinite range of useful and unexpected features to supporting gizmos. Enter the age of the Swiss Army gadget.

Online Communications – Yes, small businesses with a global or virtualized workforce could pay for dedicated videoconferencing solutions, or even high-end 3D telepresence solutions offered by the likes of **Sony** and **Teliris**. But right off the shelf, numerous smartphones and tablets like the Google Nexus S and the Asus Eee Pad Transformer Prime tablet come with dual cameras and video calling features built in. And of course, the iPhone 4S' **FaceTime** function makes video calling a snap. Enterprises on a budget can also turn to TVs that support free Skype video chats via compatible webcams, while **Cisco's TelePresence** offers a quickly accessible way to connect team members scattered across the nation too. While all require a stable, high-speed broadband Internet connection and a not inconsiderable cash outlay, going forward, solutions such as these increasingly promise to aid considerably in facilitating face-to-face communications without tanking your travel budget.

Cloud Computing – While we've yet to see users gravitate en masse towards Google's Chrome operating system, which puts the emphasis on Web-, not desktop-based applications, more devices are coming prepackaged with or offering downloadable access to individual services which store and process data remotely. Allowing remote staffers to more readily collaborate on group projects, updates to be filed and reflected in real-time right from the field, and information to be shared amongst distant parties, the trend will only become more widespread in the future. Though there are notable upsides (remote emergency backup, ready information sharing, synchronicity across locales) and downsides (privacy, security, data retrieval should a service terminate, etc.) alike associated with these options in the immediate, realize. The future of productivity lies with a desktop that travels everywhere you go, and can be pulled up wherever the need for work strikes, regardless of whether you're cruising at 30,000 feet or sunning yourself in the Hamptons.

Best Cloud Computing Services for Business

Cloud computing services, which store and crunch data on remote computer networks, then beam it back to a multitude of devices over the Internet on-command, promise to revolutionize how we work and play. With no software to purchase and install, and ready scalability, cloud computing is perfect for small and growing businesses. Splitting the difference between online storage and streaming media, here are several of the best cloud computing services for both enterprises and entrepreneurs.

Amazon Cloud Drive

What It Does: A virtual storage locker that remotely and safely houses movies, documents and photos, and streams data (including music) straight to PCs, tablets or smartphones.

Best For: Casual listeners and everyday professional desktop users, who are provided 5GB of free storage for archiving thousands of pictures, albums and files, optionally upgradeable to 1000GB of data for virtual hoarders.

Killer App: Entrepreneurs who prefer working to a backing beat will appreciate that Amazon MP3 purchases can be automatically backed up to it, then beamed down nearly anytime on-demand via Web, Android device or the Kindle Fire eReader.

Windows Live SkyDrive

What it Does: Like Amazon Cloud Drive, serves as a digital archival solution that allows users to upload, edit and save files, then access them from a Web browser on-command. A handy tool for group sharing and collaboration, the service also lets users dictate whether files are private, accessible to contacts online, or available for public viewing.

Best For: Business users who need more than the 5GB of free storage offered by Amazon Cloud Drive – Windows Live SkyDrive gives you 25GB of online backup space free. Virtualized teams will additionally appreciate the option to share files and collaborate with coworkers, customers, etc. while working remotely.

Killer App: Integration with **Microsoft Web Apps**, which allows you to upload, create, edit and share Microsoft Office documents in a Web browser.

Zoho

What It Does: Provides an alternative to desktop productivity suites like Microsoft Office, offering a range of online word processing, project management, spreadsheet, and database tools.

Best For: Business travelers and mobile professionals, who can seamlessly collaborate, share data and track progress over the Internet, no matter how distant colleagues are.

Killer App: Surprisingly affordable prices. Also, added compatibility with Microsoft Office, including optional plug-ins to bridge the platforms so you can jump between computer and cloud.

Dropbox

What It Does: Holds massive amounts of data of all types – videos, slideshows, documents, etc. – in folders that are synchronized across computers and smartphones. Update once and you update everywhere.

Best For: Frequent fliers or businesses that need to collaborate remotely or share large files, and still want to have access to data even when not connected online.

Killer App: Works on dozens of devices and a multitude of platforms, including Mac, Windows, iOS gadgets, BlackBerry, Android and even Linux. So much for "accidentally" leaving work back at the office.

Google Apps

What it Does: Provides an extensive suite of apps that allows you to store nearly any type of file (and enjoy excellent mobile access), or create and share documents, presentations, calendars and spreadsheets with minimal fuss.

Best For: Budget-minded businesses that need an affordable, one-stop online solution for basic day-to-day digital needs, or accessible way to quickly create websites, group wikis or free email addresses.

Killer App: Featured selections can be accessed from nearly any mobile device, computer or mobile browser. (Caveat: To access and stream music files, you must be on a computer desktop or one of Google's own Android-powered devices.)

Chapter 14
HIGH-TECH SERVICES AND GADGETS: GREAT MONEY SAVERS

L et's face it – running a business is not for the financially faint-of-heart. And the pressure to stay at the top of the technology game can seem daunting, especially given the current economic climate: Is all of this high-tech equipment really necessary? Needless to say, determining what's truly a must-buy vs. expensive luxury can be difficult.

Relax, though: As any well-informed techie knows, savvy use of the Web and online services can actually save you a bundle. From free and affordable apps and software to services designed especially for the needs of 21st-century businesses, here's how you can use technology to minimize overhead and operating expenses.

Enhancing Productivity

Accounting programs, day planners, even fax machines… if there's a commercial version, there's also a free substitute. Start by swiping a gratis email account from Gmail; free virus scanning courtesy of **AVG** or **Avast**; and **OpenOffice** (OpenOffice.org)'s no-charge bundle of Microsoft Office-compatible word processing, spreadsheet, database and presentation tools. Afterwards, check out **Zoho** (Zoho.com)'s online application suite, covering everything from invoicing to project management and note taking, or share schedules and information with distant colleagues using **Google Apps** (google.com/apps) or free fax service **FaxZero.com**. Finally, since time is money, save with timekeeping apps that allow you to log actions and manage tasks for maximum efficiency. Available at a reasonable cost, programs like **On Core Time Master** for iOS allow you to sort, start and stop individual tasks, or group them by individual clients. (You can also track expenses and import files into the app.) Alternative **Timesheet** for Android is a bit pared down compared to some other options out there, but offers a decent way to track projects, add breaks and create notes for businesses that don't need complicated management features.

Saving on Equipment Costs

Save on equipment costs by using hardware you already have in a creative way. Need to do a video shoot? Use an iPad and a teleprompter app (ranging from $2-$15) like **Prompterous HD** and **Teleprompt+**. Alternately, turn your smartphone into a pointer and controller for PowerPoint or Keynote presentations with the **PointerRemote** app. Or record and send voice messages via solutions such as the **Voice Recorder** (Android) or **iTalk Recorder** (iPhone) applications. It's amazing what today's gadgets can double as. Armed with as little as a smartphone and tablet, you can field salespeople, customer service reps, etc. by the dozen without even having to have an office. (A task made even easier by **Regus**'s business centers, available in multiple cities, where you can arrange for a secretary, conference rooms, mail delivery or access to business equipment while traveling as needed.) If you'd like to accept credit card payment but can't afford the huge up-front cost of merchant service equipment, check out **Square** too, which allows you to take card payments through a small card reader you attach to your iOS device. (You pay per transaction.) If you're not prepared to purchase a fax machine but have clients/contacts that rely on faxing, see options like **eFax** (compatible with multiple devices) or try the **mBox Fax & Voice** app (free) as well. The latter allows you to receive faxes and voicemails on your iPhone or iPod Touch.

Generating Brand Awareness and Marketing

Often a large part of any business's expenses, marketing is a lot more affordable in this increasingly tech-savvy era. You can establish yourself as a major player and valuable source of information in your field with a company blog, which you can easily build via free services like **Blogger** and **WordPress**. Afterwards, film and stream live video to your website or Facebook and Twitter accounts for free with your smartphone or tablet, using the **Ustream** or **SocialCam** apps (for iOS) or **Ustream Android** app. Also take advantage of the location-based social networking craze by marketing to people via **Foursquare**, **Google Plus**, **Yelp** and other popular services. It's free to list your business on these networks; once users "check in" at your location, they can receive special deals and discounts on your service or product. A tip: Consider creating to-do lists for Foursquare users to explore your virtual location. Another way to take marketing directly to the consumer is to use daily deal services like **Woot**, **1 Sale a Day** and **Daily Steals**.

Creating a Favorable Impression

Whether you're interacting with clients or potential networking resources, you always want to come off as professional and prepared. Services like **eVoice** let you set up a toll-free 888 number with a customized secretary's greeting and extensions, which adds to the professionalism of your company's image. For local, international and toll-free conference calls with optional recording, or the ability to conduct online meetings with screen-sharing capabilities, you can turn to **FreeConferenceCall.com**'s cost-effective suite of services as well. Additionally, contact information transfer apps are great for those who don't have or want to use traditional business cards. These apps send contact information directly to the inboxes and phones of your contacts, providing a convenient and conversation-starting option for networking at conferences, coffee shops, airports, etc. Check out **BeamME**, which works with the iPhone, Blackberry, Android, WiFi-enabled computers, and more. It allows you to track every contact you've made, and the vCard (electronic business card) integrates with LinkedIn, Facebook and other social networks. Another helpful contact transfer app for iPhone is **SnapDat**, which offers customizable graphically-enhanced vCards ("SnapCards"). SnapDat allows you to create as many different cards as you want so that you can customize different cards for different types of contacts.

Chapter 15
SAVE MORE MONEY: BEST FREE AND LOW-COST SOFTWARE SOLUTIONS

As veteran business owners know, software costs can skyrocket the larger your organization grows. Historically, this left professionals whose work demanded the use of commercial application suites with three solutions: Scale revenues accordingly, find cheaper yet less full-featured alternatives or dabble in the shady world of software piracy. But luckily for today's enterprise, there's a new option entirely – download a wealth of free or low-cost software programs that offer just as much functionality as favorite high-end desktop packages at zero or next to no cost. Looking to login to a world of instant savings? The following solutions, each readily retrievable right from your Internet browser, quickly pay dividends.

Anti-Virus and Spyware

Viruses, trojans and spyware can quickly bring your business to its knees. Thankfully, you needn't take out a costly annual subscription to stop them cold. **AVG Anti-Virus Free Edition** provides a comfortable basic level of protection, complete with regular updates, that's enough to keep your computer operating at peak performance. **Avira AntiVir Personal** also boasts reliable threat detection rates, while **avast! Free Antivirus** further operates in real-time to prevent unauthorized attempts to modify your PC's contents. None offer the level or sheer depth of bonus features found in premium solutions such as Kaspersky Anti-Virus, McAfee Web & Email Protection or Norton Anti-Virus. But all do deliver a degree of security that's perfectly suitable for everyday use.

Communications

Skype, which is now compatible with select smartphone systems and TVs in addition to desktop/laptop computers, allows you to make affordable international calls, and videoconference free of charge. Used in tandem with complementary email services like **Gmail**, **Windows Live Mail** and **Yahoo Mail** (many of which also offer calendar, photo and file sharing features) it's easy to stay in touch with customers and partners. Mozilla's **Thunderbird** e-mail client makes a great substitute for Microsoft Outlook as well, with its flexibility, speedy response times and intuitive setup. Note that blogging services such as **Blogger** and **WordPress** further allow you to publish your own websites and magazines, building community all the while. Social network and instant messaging fans can additionally look to a host of desktop and smartphone apps such as **TweetDeck**, **Digsby** and **Seesmic** for all their communications needs.

Multimedia

Pricey as Adobe's industry-leading PhotoShop can be, any professional who needs the ability to edit, crop and touch-up images to modern publishing standards will find graphic editing toolkit **GIMP** a worthy pro bono alternative. **IrfanView** also lets you view graphics in virtually any format, and makes it easy to adjust and convert images as needed. In need of images, music, or video for your projects? Check out **CreativeCommons**, a clearinghouse of creative works licensed for public use, and **Flickr** provides millions of searchable royalty-free images. Crowdsourced design sites, such as **Crowdspring**, **99Designs**, and **DesignCrowd** are also great tools for creating a winning logo, website or graphic design project at minimum expense. For those looking to build podcasts, **Audacity** provides a great audio recording and editing solution with a powerful range of functions, though the initial learning curve can take time to master. Prefer working with video footage? A range of film editing packages such as **iMovie** and **JumpCut** make it easy to create video packages. Anyone needing to capture videos of their desktop for tutorial or training purposes should also look to **TipCam** or **CamStudio** for an all-purpose recording solution. Note: **ImgBurn** ranks among the best CD, DVD and Blu-ray burning applications for sharing your creations when done.

GIMP is an excellent image-editing program if you don't have the bucks to shell out for Photoshop

Productivity

Microsoft Office 2010's suite of **Office Web Apps** offers some free options for sharing, retrieving and editing documents, spreadsheets and presentations anywhere. However, other cloud computing solutions such as **Zoho** and **Google Docs** prove just as worthy alternatives, and have been in more widespread use for a longer period of time. Still, by far the most popular solution for those seeking to work with common workplace file formats and types is **OpenOffice**. While you'll sacrifice some features native to more robust (and expensive) commercial desktop packages such as in-depth formatting and style controls, fret not: For most tasks, these simple solutions will easily suffice, saving you hundreds, if not thousands, of software licensing fees in the process. Also be certain to check out **Evernote**, which lets you create and clip virtual notes, allowing you to easily assemble and browse a list of things to do, intriguing websites and items to purchase.

Storage

Dropbox remains our clear-cut favorite for storing, sharing and retrieving files amongst multiple users and PCs, allowing you to backup and access projects housed on a remote server on-demand. Up to 2GB of storage is offered with a free signup, and it makes a tremendously effective way for groups to synchronize data, then collaborate on and edit projects or monitor their ongoing progress. However, **Google Drive** now offers 5GB of free, synchronized cross-platform storage and group editing and collaboration tools as well. **Box.com** also offers similar services, as does **Windows Live SkyDrive** (also on **iPhone**), which provides users with a whopping 25GB of storage that can be password protected for private access. Hate having e-mails bounce back because attachments are too large, but just need a quick, one-time solution? **YouSendIt** can help, letting you send a single file of up to 2GB in size (or whole folders) as a simple webpage link. For a helpful synchronization service, try **FreeFileSync**, an easy-to-use and versatile software that should please both new and experienced users.

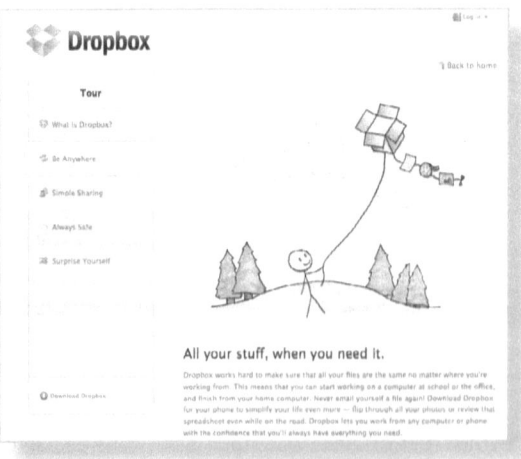

Dropbox is one of several free online storage services that let you backup, share and access files from anywhere.

Chapter 16
MUST-HAVE GADGETS FOR BUSINESS OWNERS

C all it information overload. Despite a massive array of must-see high-tech product launches in virtually every category from smartphones to eReaders and connected devices, let's be honest: In an age where "newer," "faster" and "shinier" are less simple adjectives than cultural imperatives, it's enough to make even the most gadget-savvy business owner's head short circuit.

Thankfully for your organization, though, many of today's increasingly portable, online-connected electronics make a great fit for professionals at every career level. Using them, you can not only empower your business by allowing staffers to access Web pages, emails, documents, presentations, calendars and contacts from nearly anywhere. Coupled with cutting-edge advances in mobile technology, it's also possible to unchain yourself from your desk entirely and instantly retrieve your workspace on the go, letting your entire team effortlessly stay in contact and collaborate with distant colleagues on-demand. Still more devices offer added benefits such as the ability to safely store and transport data in pocket-size packages, while other gizmos make sharing multimedia or conversing with customers easy. As such, today's business owner has never had a more powerful set of tools for connecting and communicating at their fingertips.

But across the board, whether they offer upsides ranging from turn-by-turn directions to cloud file storage or support for recording your own viral video marketing spots, all come with the same drawback: These devices are only as effective as you let them be. Following are five must-have gadgets that every modern professional should own – and everything you need to know to really make the most of them.

1 Smartphones – Cell phones so powerful they can practically serve as laptop replacements, these handheld devices are today's top electronic productivity tool for mobile professionals. Wielding one, you can surf the Internet; send/receive emails; share audio, video and photos; teleconference; and add endless functionality from invoice tracking to image editing using downloadable software applications known as "apps."

Available in an array of technical configurations, feature readouts and operating systems though, here's the catch – there's no one-size-fits-all solution. For example: Some users prefer handsets with physical QWERTY keyboards (e.g., RIM's BlackBerry Bold 9900/9930), which make sending e-mails and text messages easier. Others don't mind trading a virtual keyboard for a clumsier on-screen one if it means gaining access to multimedia recording features and being able to quickly access social networks (see: Apple's iPhone 4S). Similarly, a model such as the Motorola ATRIX 4G might tempt power users who need to seamlessly integrate with their favorite online services.

Some confusion here is inevitable: Loading and connection speeds differ between models, as do compatibility with wireless networks and enterprise email solutions. Hardware components such as touchscreens and digital/video cameras are also of variable configuration and quality, with a panoply of exotically-named operating systems (Android, iOS, Windows Phone, etc.) powering various units. The key here: Go hands-on with any device before purchasing, and check each carrier's cellular coverage maps to ensure you're never without decent download speeds or signal bars.

Take a good, close look at each phone's capabilities and ask yourself: Do I need the ability to multitask between programs, or are 4G LTE speeds and a built-in video camera for filming HD promo spots for easy upload to YouTube more important? Is a GPS with free turn-by-turn directions a necessity given how often you're on the road traveling between appointments, or the ability to edit Word, Excel and PowerPoint files more crucial? Each option comes with tradeoffs, but as with any personal assistant, it pays to choose the one that best suits your profession and personality.

2 Laptops, Tablets and Ultrabooks – While there's no replacing a desktop or all-in-one PC when it comes to pure horsepower and speed, realize that given their versatile nature and mobility, systems such as laptops, ultrabooks (super-slim, yet powerful notebooks) and tablets (touchscreen slates) can oftentimes make perfectly worthy secondary systems or set-top substitutes. (Skip netbooks – low-cost units that skimp on power and performance to provide cost-savings – where possible, given that falling prices mean that you can increasingly buy higher-powered, lightweight systems for less with each passing year.) Thank small sizes and weights, which render them simple to stuff in a carry-on or pack along when you visit colleagues a couple floors up. Most importantly, however, such systems offer ample power for everyday routine tasks like sending email, browsing the Web or word processing. In other words, they offer the option to only purchase as much PC as you really need.

There's no sense breaking the bank here either, unless you're working on hardware-intensive projects such as video editing or desktop publishing that require high-end features like dedicated 3D graphics cards and premium CPUs. The good news being that for eight out of every 10 routine tasks, multiple manufacturers from Acer to Sony, Dell, Lenovo and Samsung offer affordable options at prices ranging from $400 and up. However, in a well-crowded field, there are a few standouts. Consider the Asus Zenbook, with efficient processor, high-resolution display, and added connectivity options, or Acer's Aspire S3, which packs great storage capacity and lots of power. Likewise, the Toshiba Thrive tablet also scores with its Android 3.1 OS and pre-installed practical applications.

When shopping for one, consider the most common tasks you'll use the system for on a daily basis, but don't underestimate the importance of ergonomics. While most computers in these classes can handle similar workloads, not all offer enough battery power to see you through an international flight, or are appropriate for creating extensive spreadsheets or presentations. Likewise, it's one thing to type out brief notes on units with a small keyboard – another, more painful, task entirely trying to bang out full-scale market research reports.

In terms of tablet PCs like Apple's iPad and the Samsung Galaxy Tab, value especially depends on the individual. As a rule of thumb, it's best to grab such machines only if their functionality and level of performance meet those required by your industry and can help you field common routine tasks.

3 Digital Video Cameras – Ask social media mavens and they'll tell you: Video is the new coin of the online realm. Moreover, for business owners, it's also a godsend in terms of cost-effective marketing solutions. Using an array of budget digital camcorders such as Kodak's Playfull Dual Zi12, Panasonic's HM-TA20 and Sony's Bloggie Live, anyone can become an aspiring producer. While you won't get broadcast quality results or top-caliber zoom, audio recording and image stabilization features from these gadgets, which retail for under $150-$250, consider: You still get high-definition video output that's good enough for your blog or website, and just as capable as anything of scoring millions of hits on online video aggregators like **Metacafe**, **Vimeo** or **YouTube**.

Potential applications here are endless. Using these devices, you can record behind-the-scenes footage, making-of segments, online video diaries, client testimonials, interviews with industry leaders and more. Beam feeds out live or add captured clips to your website, and it's easy to create a steady stream of content that helps breathe personality into your brand, builds viewer empathy and keeps viewers coming back for more. Similarly, by using instructional videos as a platform, you can also quickly establish yourself and your business as subject matter experts in any given space. From screening webinars and tradeshow panels for widespread distribution to creating your own documentaries, options are limited only by your imagination.

Be advised, however: Giving the increasing performance of HD video cameras found on smartphone models such as the iPhone 4S, purchasing a separate standalone unit may prove unnecessary for some.

4 Bluetooth Headsets – As often as your phone rings, it pays to invest in a noise-canceling Bluetooth headset that enables clear, hands-free calling. Such solutions aren't just practical, allowing you to quickly take calls without letting go of the wheel. They're also a vital safety measure, as increasingly stringent legislation aims to curb the rise of accidents caused by professionals attempting to talk, text or tweet while in the car.

Aliph's Jawbone Era is among the gold standards here, though Motorola's Finiti and Plantronics' Voyager Pro make good choices as well. Many even offer the option to download apps or software updates, letting you dictate notes or record voice memos on-demand. Just be certain you pick a comfortable unit that's suitable for use during extended conference calls, and one with solid battery life and noise-canceling capabilities for blocking out blaring horns and other background clatter.

5 **GPS Systems** – While the debate still rages about standalone GPS navigation systems' relevance in the face of smartphones' growing propensity for featuring powerful built-in GPS devices, here's the more important takeaway: Between the popularity of dashboard units from manufacturers like TomTom and Garmin; free, cell phone-ready solutions like Google Maps Navigation and Navigator FREE; and optional premium-priced mapping apps for a variety of handsets, everyone wins. Working professionals determined to be on time for their next appointment, no matter which city it's in, or find a decent lunch meeting spot, now have a massive array of navigational utilities at their disposal. So whether you prefer a dedicated, windshield-mountable solution with real-time traffic updates, or the convenience of simply stuffing a GPS in your pocket, beware: There's no excuse for being late for an important date again.

Looking for more specific purchasing recommendations? Following are some of the best new business gadgets on the market, as of press time.

Best Tablet PC and Laptops

HP Envy 14 Spectre – High price aside, it's hard to argue with the Gorilla Glass-clad stunner's brawny Core i5 or i7 processor, 14-inch HD screen and 9 hours of battery life, which make it equal parts workhorse and conversation piece. Be forewarned, however: Though a travel-friendly fit for road warriors hoping to fire off emails en masse or catch up on work while flying the friendly skies, its attractive looks may prompt constant comments from fellow passengers.

Also See:
Lenovo Yoga – Packs a rotating and foldable display, giving the Windows 8 machine the power to act as both a laptop and tablet PC. Offering professionals a variety of upsides – on-demand digital downloads, a convenient form factor, flexible capabilities for use in varied business situations – it could prove a solid fit for your enterprise.

Samsung Series 9 – The PC's answer to the MacBook Air, this striking machine clocks in at just half an inch thick, yet doesn't compromise on performance or computing muscle. Despite weighing half as much as the average laptop, it still offers a high-end quad-core i7 processor, brilliant 15-inch screen and panoply of ports for connecting USB drives, outputting video via HDMI cable or pulling multimedia off micro-SD cards.

Asus Eee Pad MeMO – Packing a beefy quad-core Tegra 3 graphics processor from NVIDIA, but retailing for just $249, this 7-inch Android tablet touts enough power to deliver gasp-inducing multimedia showpieces without short-circuiting your monthly budget.

Best Smartphones

Droid Razr Maxx – Slim and trim profile aside, entrepreneurs will love the phone for an even more practical reason: Massive battery life. Boasting blazing 4G LTE download speeds, yet 20+ hours of continuous talk time (including enough juice to drive from LA to Vegas and back using GPS navigation without recharging), it's hard to argue with its practical upsides. Letting you take conference calls, field emails and plot appointments without having to worry about plugging in, the handset's a potential lifesaver at meetings, tradeshows and conferences.

Also See:
Nokia Lumia 900 – Among the best new Windows Phones and initial fruits of Microsoft's much-debated partnership with Nokia, the stylishly-appointed cell phone scores with a crisp, 4.3-inch AMOLED display and brisk 4G LTE connectivity.

Samsung Galaxy Note – Is it a phone or a tablet? Hard to say, but this promising Android hybrid still wows with its 5.3-inch Super AMOLED touchscreen, productivity-enhancing stylus, 8MP camera and note-taking functions, which help mitigate worries surrounding its oversized physical footprint.

HTC Titan II – Makes capturing stunning product shots or social media-friendly images a breeze with its shockingly powerful 16MP camera, image stabilization capabilities and robust photo editing features, including redeye reduction. A burly 1.5Ghz Snapdragon processor and 4G LTE connectivity don't hurt either.

Best Video Cameras and Camcorders

Sony Bloggie Live – While it doesn't provide eye-popping special effects like the Sony MHS-FS3 Bloggie 3D (an affordable solution for capturing 3D videos), don't discount the device's coolest trick: Support for live-streaming video to the Web, complete with options to receive short messages from viewers. Translation: Powered by popular video sharing service Qik, you can beam links to live broadcasts out via Facebook, Twitter, YouTube or email straight from the field, plus let observers comment on tapings. Amusingly, features like 1080p high-def filming and a sizable 8GB internal hard drive feel almost negligible by comparison.

Also See:
Kodak Playfull Dual Zi12 – Apart from offering much-needed external microphone input (which enhances audio when filming), also captures 1080p HD video and 12MP stills, plus provides expandable SD memory card storage and effortless on-board movie-editing features.

Sony Handycam HDR-CX130 – An incredibly compact camcorder with a rotating 3.0" LCD touch-screen and 30x optical zoom. Capable of recording video in 1080p and taking 3MP images. Excellent in low light.

Nikon CoolPix S8200 – This 16 MP digital camera is capable of capturing 1080 high-def video, but really wows with a 14X optical zoom lens and Nikon's exclusive image analysis technology – perfect of capturing crystal clear images of your new office and products.

Best Gadgets and Accessories

Jawbone Era Bluetooth Headset – Popular as predecessor the Jawbone Icon was given its top performance and stylish look, this hands-free Bluetooth headset does it one better by adding motion controls. Featuring a built-in accelerometer, you can shake the device to pair it with a mobile phone, or answer calls by tapping your finger. As ever, solid noise cancellation features also make it easy to hold meetings while strolling down city streets, with high-definition audio and a 25% larger speaker further helping boost sonic clarity. Most exciting though is support for regular downloadable software updates or apps through the MyTalk platform, as developers can theoretically add an array of touch-activated features from automated note-taking to email dictation.

Also See:
Mophie Juice Pack Plus – Hate getting halfway through the workday only to find your iPhone is running on fumes? This nifty case, which doubles as a rechargeable spare battery for the iPhone 4/4S, can put you back in the game for up to 8 additional hours. The only downside: If you're using an existing case (e.g. the Hex Code Wallet, among our favorites for its professional styling), you'll have to remove it before juicing up.

SuperHero – An iPhone and iPod touch charging dock that simultaneously backs up contacts and photos to an SD memory card (4GB and up) while in the cradle so you can restore or transfer data on-demand.

GoFlex HDD – A shocking 9mm thick, this super-skinny external hard drive's USB 3.0 data-transfer times are as miniscule as its physical footprint. Compatible with Macs and PCs.

Chapter 17
ULTRABOOKS:
SHOULD YOU BUY ONE?

Much ado has recently been made over Intel's so-called "ultrabooks." Still not sure what those are? They're a line of lightweight, portable laptops that mimic a tablet's anorexic dimensions without sacrificing PC hallmarks like heavyweight performance and full-size keyboards.

But they do invite questions. For example, is the ultrabook simply a rebranding of an existing computer category? Maybe. But they're powerful and portable, so the real question is, should you invest in them?

Priced between $900-1500 on average as of press time and offered in myriad shapes and sizes—including Gorilla Glass-encased units, hybrids, and clamshell models—current ultrabook options are designed to target every flavor of enterprise and working professional. Notable choices include:

HP Envy 14 Spectre – A striking–and strikingly expensive ($1399)–14-inch beauty packing 9 hours of battery life that offers a hefty Core i5 or i7 processor, multi-touch capability, and rapid-start performance for enhanced productivity.

Lenovo Yoga – This Windows 8 machine doubles as both laptop and tablet courtesy of a swiveling/folding display. It's a great example of just one of many possible ultrabook form factors to come.

Dell XPS 13 – Splits the difference between eye-catching design and everyday performance, marrying an aluminum body and attractive 13.3-inch monitor with enterprise-level service and TPM security for IT professionals. A 128-256 GB solid state drive for dependable data backup is an added bonus.

Samsung Series 9 – Crams a beefy quad-core i7 processor, bright 15-inch screen, and multitude of ports (USB, HDMI, micro-SD memory card, etc.) into a half-inch thick frame that weighs only 2.5 pounds. Just one catch: The not-so-bargain $1499 price tag.

Note that while initial suggested retail prices may seem prohibitive, they should fall considerably in coming months. Both overall selection and potential business applications will also improve considerably, as manufacturers and software makers alike increasingly exploit flexible designs to deliver new and noteworthy hardware uses.

Weighing an ultrabook vs. a tablet for your mobile workforce?

Here are the pros:

Physical Keyboards – Unlike tablets, whose virtual typepads are ill-suited to penning lengthy business plans, pitches, and sales reports, ultrabooks offer traditional, full-size keypads.

Larger Screens – Ultrabooks offer larger displays better suited for desktop sharing, product demos, and presentations. The greater visual real estate also makes multitasking in several windows and teleconferencing easier.

Faster CPUs and GPUs – Packing Intel's celebrated processors for speedy number-crunching and enhanced visual performance, ultrabooks (most notably Ivy Bridge models) can power more robust and feature-laden software programs than tablets.

Greater Compatibility – Despite the massive selection of apps provided for smartphones and tablets, as true Windows PCs, ultrabooks offer compatibility with the widest range of cloud and Web apps, online services, and desktop utilities available.

Now, the cons:

If portability and price are most important, a tablet may be all you need. Have you seen the $249 Tegra 3 chip-powered Asus Eee Pad MeMO 370T? The 7-inch tablet will offer everyday utility (Web surfing, email, etc.), performance computing and slick multimedia playback for pennies. Consider it indicative of where the market's headed.

Existing choices neither greatly push the computing envelope nor do they generally come with nifty extras like high-end video cards or Blu-ray drives.

Provided you don't mind packing a few extra pounds, or cramming chunkier models into a carry-on, standard-issue laptops can be had for hundreds less.

Who they're best for

Ultrabooks are a solid fit for road warriors, social media mavens, and start-up staffs with serious multimedia needs. They offer employees portability, versatility, and access to sleek, powerful systems. And they don't force you to compromise on productivity due to program incompatibilities or fat fingers.

The Lenovo Yoga features
a swivel display

Chapter 18
GO-GO GADGETS:
MOBILE DEVICES AND TECHNOLOGIES

Money's always a concern for entrepreneurs, but as limited resources come, time can often be just as pertinent. Thankfully, a number of go-go gadgets and high-tech services designed for road warriors can help mobile business owners boost productivity while on the move.

In-Car Apps and Online Connectivity

Car owners looking to stay connected have several choices.

Ford's SYNC with MyFordTouch hands-free, voice activated technology is presently available in over three million vehicles including the 2011 Taurus and Explorer, and 2012 Focus and Mustang. In addition to enjoying a color-coded dashboard display with dual 4.2" LCD monitors for quickly accessing turn-by-turn directions or retrieving your phonebook for hands-free calling, you can also dictate tweets or change radio stations via spoken command.

Toyota offers an in-dash multimedia system called Entune too, which pairs with smartphone apps so you can conduct online searches via Bing, book lunch meetings through **OpenTable** or access traffic reports and stock quotes. Other auto manufacturers including General Motors, Ford, Mercedes-Benz, Audi and Nissan also offer support for iPhone and Android handsets or downloadable apps, as do in-car entertainment providers like Alpine and Pioneer.

OnStar even offers a **MyLink app** that lets you turn your phone into a remote control for your Cadillac, Chevrolet, GMC or Buick. Using it, you can unlock your door, start the vehicle or activate your horn and lights from a distance.

Hands-Free Calling and Bluetooth Headsets

A number of high-quality hands-free calling and wireless Bluetooth headsets also make it easy to conduct meetings or converse with colleagues while behind the wheel.

Consider the **MoGo Talk XD and XD2**, which rank among the more practical, as in addition to offering four hours of talk time and noise and wind reduction features, their earpieces snap directly into a compatible iPhone case. Given this specialized housing, it's extremely difficult to lose the devices.

Still, those looking for premium audio quality or a more stylish solution can try the **Motorola H17txt** with MotoSpeak, whose dual microphones do an excellent job of filtering out ambient background noise.

The **Platronics Savior M1100** has also earned praise from reviewers for its three microphones and excellent sound caliber. Added enhancements include the Plantronics Vocalist service (one year free with purchase), which lets you use voice-activated commands to send email and texts, or listen to breaking news.

GPS, Outdoor and Location-Based Devices

Those who frequently travel off the grid to remote areas might also consider picking up the **Spot Connect**. A puck-shaped navigator that connects your smartphone to communications satellites, it offers instant location tracking, and the option to check in with the office anywhere, regardless of local cellular coverage.

Paired with the **Spark Tablet PC Case**, a lightweight, waterproof solar charger that stores a full charge for your iPad or Samsung Galaxy Tab with exposure to sunlight, you're ready to do remote fieldwork.

Should the need to capture on-site images for research, fact-finding or insurance purposes arise, Pentax's **Optio WG-1 GPS** digital camera can help as well. A rugged 14MP model with video recording features that's water-, cold- and shock-proof, plus resistant to drops and crushing, it includes GPS geo-tagging features, so you can quickly catalogue images with your location.

Presentation and Public Speaking Tools

Portable presentation tools are also a must for any mobile operative.

Case in point: Want to scribble information down on a page then watch it suddenly appear on a computer screen? Wireless solution **Papershow** can make the dream a reality. Simply hoist the system's Bluetooth digital pen, scribble on a piece of interactive paper and your doodles appear on a Mac or PC courtesy of a wireless USB connector.

While a more expensive solution for displaying sales pitches or market forecasts, the **Sony Handycam HDR-PJ50V** also promises to save you from carrying multiple gadgets. A combination two-in-one 1080p HD video camera and projector, it can record over 90 hours of board meetings, presentations and product demos on a built-in 220GB hard drive. Once captured, the hybrid device can display up to 60" (diagonal screen) images on-command, allowing trainers or social media gurus to instantly conduct impromptu screenings.

Papershow allows a digital pen to simultaneously display handwritten notes on your computer.

Chapter 19
BEST BUSINESS SMARTPHONES AND BUYING TIPS

t's your friend, your constant companion, your sole source of comfort on the road… even your colleague and confidante. We're talking, of course, about your smartphone – that magic hybrid device that serves as equal parts mobile communications center, day planner and personal assistant. Capable of functioning as any entrepreneur's home away from their desk, today's cloud computing-friendly and 3G/4G high-speed Internet-enabled cellular handsets literally make it possible to take the office everywhere you go.

But with so many options from virtually every carrier, and an equally astounding array of features – touchscreen displays, streaming audio/video, units capable of doubling as standalone HD video cameras, etc. – to pick from, which to choose? In many ways, it's a Catch 22 for working professionals. Given the wealth of selections now on offer, there are a staggering number of options designed to suit a similarly dizzying array of individual needs and tastes. Nor is every operating system created equal in terms of juggling contacts, enjoying third-party support from independent software makers and managing key functions such as syncing with high-end email servers. In other words, caveat emptor: Picking the right cell phone for business use is a lot like dating. From price point to cosmetic styling and overall functionality, there's a handset for everyone out there – and a lot of fish in the sea.

Start by asking yourself what matters most to you individually. Is it the option to juggle multiple email accounts or high-speed Web surfing? Freedom to browse and edit sales presentations and budget forecasts at will, or the means to provide hours of blissful distraction as you hop a red-eye from LAX to JFK? Only you can decide which features are most attractive, and tradeoffs worth making, in order to spend countless days, weeks and all-nighters on end married to a potential device. Although thankfully, in fairness, should the need arise, breaking up is much easier (if no less painful) dependent on the length of any guaranteed cell phone service contract you've signed as a means of subsidizing the initial purchase.

When searching for the model which best suit your needs, a few words of advice, though. It's imperative that you always go hands-on with any given unit before purchasing, and research compatibility with your organization's present infrastructure and IT backbone. Sourcing real-world feedback from colleagues and friends is also vital, lest you inadvertently discover your office to be a Bermuda Triangle-esque dead zone from which no call can enter or escape. A number of general points worth considering when judging potential candidates follow as well.

Battery Life – Just a couple sessions into a lengthy tradeshow or worse – at 2AM while driving in circles looking for your hotel – you don't want to find yourself sprinting for the nearest power outlet. So do yourself a favor: Choose a phone rated for 4-5 hours of talk time minimum, and one that offers a portable charger suitable for quick stowaway during travel at that. Springing for an extended battery is often a wise investment too, as is keeping a laptop handy in case a quick USB-powered recharge is needed.

Internet Access – Ask yourself: How fast does the phone browse the Web, download apps and videos, and retrieve email attachments? Units all offer different surfing and download performance, as do cell phone carriers themselves. High-speed capability is often also limited to specific regions, with major urban centers such as Atlanta and San Francisco able to access better and faster connections than remotely-situated areas. While 3G networks may suffice for everyday tasks and browsing sites optimized for mobile devices, faster 4G access is a must for heavy Web surfers, multimedia enthusiasts and those looking to download sizable new applications.

Calling Plans and Coverage – From unlimited data access to free text messaging, complimentary nights and weekends and discounts for multiple devices that share a single plan, a number of piecemeal and all-you-can-eat options are available by carrier. Keep in mind, though: Certain handsets are exclusive to specific providers, which may limit your choices. When choosing a plan, it's also best not to overdo it – you can always add features if you find yourself going above your monthly minute allotment or receiving an unexpected volume of text messages from coworkers. To estimate how much call time to spring for on an ongoing basis, take a look back at your business' cell phone bills for the last 6-12 months, and average monthly minute usage. Be sure to check your provider's coverage map (available at its homepage) to ensure that there's a geographic match to minimize potential roaming charges and outages as well. International calling support should additionally be considered by those who commonly travel overseas.

Miscellaneous Features – Other options to consider when shopping for a smartphone for business use include:

QWERTY Keyboard – A boon for those whose lives revolve around email and text messaging.

WiFi Connectivity – Allows you to tap into nearby high-speed wireless Internet hotspots and, in some cases, even make free or heavily discounted calls.

GPS – Provides mobile navigation services for on-the-go travelers seeking local maps or step-by-step directions to their next business appointment.

Password Access and Email Encryption – For added security and data loss prevention.

Contacts and Calendars – An extensive address book and the ability to synchronize schedules and contacts between devices are powerful productivity tools.

Word, Excel and PDF Support – Enables you to read or edit common business document, spreadsheet and presentation formats.

Touchscreen Display – Provides enhanced multimedia features and a more intuitive user interface.

Cloud and Streaming Capabilities – Remote data storage that allows you to upload, organize and share all types of files, or stream multimedia down on command.

As for which models come recommended, see as follows. Just the tip of the iceberg in terms of what's available in the smartphone market, all provide a welcome starting point for today's entrepreneur.

Droid Razr Maxx – Delivers insane battery life, letting you speak continuously with clients and colleagues for over 20 hours, or enjoy GPS navigation capabilities that won't sputter out in the middle of length road trips. That the handset is also as slim and trim as predecessors, yet more ruggedized and capable of taking a beating, makes a nice plus too, as does breezy 4G LTE high-speed connectivity. Keeping you from having to suddenly sprint for a power outlet or worry about missing vital emails or instant messages while traveling or attending tradeshows, make no mistake. What it lacks in eye-popping gimmicks, the phone more than makes up for in pure practicality.

Google Nexus S – Earns high marks for its Android 2.3 Gingerbread OS with fully-integrated Google Voice, 4G speeds and 4" Super AMOLED display. Also includes Wi-Fi, Bluetooth, and an integrated GPS. Its 3G/4G hotspot capability allows you to host up to five wireless devices. For videoconferencing, the handset features a 5MP rear camera with front-facing webcam. It also boasts near field communication (NFC) capability, which allows wireless transactions and data exchange between mobile devices, as well as contactless credit card payment.

Motorola Droid 2 Global – This truly global smartphone is incredibly secure and can be used as a mobile hotspot for up to five devices. Quad-band GSM capabilities allow you to send and receive emails and calls from abroad. Business travelers will also appreciate VZ navigator, Skype Mobile, Visual Voice Mail, V Cast, and tons of Google apps pre-installed on the device. It also comes with three multi-region charging adaptors. Other notable features include the Android 2.2 OS, a slider QWERTY keyboard, 3.7" touchscreen, 5MP rear-facing camera, and 1.2 GHz processor with GPU.

Apple iPhone 4S – Virtual keyboard (beware near-death experiences while barreling down the freeway and attempting to dial) and enterprise-level shortcomings aside, still worth recommending. Thank premium download speeds, a user-friendly front end, massive multimedia support and countless downloadable apps that provide everything from free calling to mileage tracking, sales support and local bus schedules. Love that GPS as well: Google Maps has saved us from being late to more than one meeting. The 8MP rear-facing camera with LED flash records 1080p HD video, and features easy, one-tap videoconferencing with **FaceTime**. Backed by Apple's newest operating system, iOS 5, the phone additionally offers improved notifications, voice-controlled assistant Siri, and the ability to save email contacts, schedules, photos, etc. to the Web. And compatibility with **iCloud** allows you to store and synchronize your music, photos, apps, mail, contacts, documents, etc. across all your mobile devices.

Nokia Lumia 900 – Among the top showpieces from Microsoft's well-publicized partnership with Nokia, the handset's specs don't necessarily wow on paper, despite upsides which include a 1.4Ghz CPU and 4G LTE connectivity for improved download speeds. But seeing is believing, with a dazzling 4.3-inch AMOLED display powering enhanced day-to-day program usage and productivity-enhancing Windows Phone applications a big plus, as is the device's 8MP camera with dual-LED flash. Coupled with the Lumia 900's eye-catching design, it all adds up to a solid performer that serves as an obvious centerpiece for the corporate titans' combined efforts.

Samsung Galaxy Note – Larger than your average smartphone, but providing less visual real-estate than the average tablet PC, it's hard to say exactly where this hybrid falls in terms of target audience. But with a 5.3-inch Super AMOLED touchscreen delivering sharp visuals, stylus-powered note taking capabilities and ready support for snapping photos or capturing voice recordings built-in, the Android model definitely has promise. Those seeking a mix of portability and performance may find it a solid fit, as a lightweight design and presentation-friendly features provide significant upsides for road warriors seeking an alternative that sits somewhere between existing mobile devices.

Motorola Atrix 4G – One of the best of the AT&T Android models, this phone features a dual-core processor, a 5 megapixel camera, a front-facing camera for video calls, and an HDMI port. With its laptop and desktop docks, it can actually substitute for either as well – an ideal feature for the business traveler. The quarter HD screen allows you to get much more out of content-heavy applications, although there's no 1080p HD video recording or playback. Even so, the speed, versatility, and high-end features of the Motorola Atrix 4G make it a great option.

The Nokia Lumia 900

Chapter 20
ALL ABOUT APPS: 10 BEST BUSINESS APPS FOR SMARTPHONES AND TABLETS

No matter your weapon of choice from iPhone to iPad, BlackBerry or Android device, apps make every entrepreneur's life that much easier. But with thousands available for download on dozens of mobile gadgets, it can be hard to tell which are really worth their weight in microchips. Following are 10 of the top business apps for entrepreneurs to help you get started, all of which put the power to boost productivity right in the palm of your hand.

Springpad – Organize, share and save collected ideas and information. Springpad automatically categorizes everything you save and provides unique organizational features like adding tags and creating notebooks. It also sends you customized updates based on your interests (price drops, news, product availability, etc.). Ideal for the on-the-go traveler who wants to remember contacts, business locations, product specs, etc.

Evernote – Ever feel like the absent-minded professor? Try taming professional clutter with a service that lets you take virtual memos on-demand. Capable of storing text, photos and voice recordings, you can dictate, snap pictures and automatically synchronize updates across your computer, smartphone and tablet, or even tag notes by location. It helps you stay on top of tasks despite constantly being pulled in 300 directions.

Scanner Pro – Instantly transforms your iPhone into a portable, multi-page document scanner than can capture electronic copies of invoices, business cards and signed documents. From meeting notes to contracts, its automatic edge detection and high-quality image processing capabilities readily handle conversions. Letting you produce and skim e-mail-ready PDFs on-demand, you can also set custom page sizes or password-protect files for added security.

Flight Track Pro – Staying on top of flight delays and gate changes is easy with this handy travel tracker. Import trip data from an airline confirmation email, and it'll monitor your itinerary, alerting you to delays, cancellations and alternate boarding plans. The program also provides satellite and weather imagery, and maps of airport terminals if case you need to sprint for a connection.

MightyMeeting – Upload presentations and product videos to the cloud then access them nearly anytime, anywhere with this handy demonstration tool. Allowing you to quickly call up clips and slideshows on your smartphone or tablet PC, it makes it easy to showcase sales pitches or market overviews on-demand. Users can also connect mobile devices to a widescreen projector for added impact.

Gist – Lets you organize and update contacts in a single location with minimal fuss. Capable of importing email, phone and address data from multiple sources (inbox, social network, smartphone, etc), the program makes it simple to keep up with acquaintances' ever-shifting details. Options to view colleagues' running Facebook and Twitter feeds without exiting the program, well… That's just an added bonus.

AroundMe – Frequently find yourself on the road and wishing you could find a good restaurant? Or a close gas station? AroundMe identifies your position and gives you a list of businesses in whatever category you select. Featured categories include bank, bar, gas station, hospital, hotel, movie theater, restaurant, supermarket, theater and taxi.

Print n Share – Dream of printing right from your smartphone or tablet PC? Wish granted. Wielding this nifty app, you can send documents straight to a WiFi printer, or one connected to a Mac or PC. Requests may also be issued remotely over 3G wireless networks, so you can pick up copies of contracts or insertion orders the next time you breeze by HQ.

Jump Desktop – Offers the option to control your desktop remotely, regardless of where business takes you. Armed with an Internet connection, you can manipulate files or folders via touchscreen, and actively browse your home or work computer. Compatible with Mac and PC systems, it's a useful way to stay productive without having to pack a hernia-inducing laptop along for any voyage.

OmniFocus – More expensive than most apps, but cheaper than an executive assistant, this full suite of utilities for task management makes plotting a daily agenda much simpler. Capable of organizing tasks by groups, contexts, tools, locations and resources, it helps you keep tabs on ongoing engagements and prioritize to-do lists. Add in support for synchronizing between multiple devices, and it's powerful enough to offset most entrepreneurs' inborn ADD.

Mighty Meeting allows you to pitch from the web, your tablet or smartphone

43 Life-Saving Apps and Gadgets for Entrepreneurs

Of all the problems which plague small business owners, technology issues can be among the most embarrassing. From smartphones which suddenly die in the middle of pitches to unexpected software crashes and missing or incompatible PowerPoint presentations, every entrepreneur's been there, though.

Given that disaster's unavoidable, veteran IT experts know that it pays to be proactive. Thankfully, with a little help from leading apps, gadgets and online services, there's no excuse for today's high-tech executive to ever be caught unprepared again. Buy or download the following tools, and you'll always be prepared for the worst the working world has to offer.

Battery Life and Backup – Popular as Apple's iPhone 4 and 4S have become with business owners, each has a dirty secret. Battery life tops out between 4-6 hours of talk time and Internet, making charge-extending cases like mophie's **Juice Pack Plus** and MiLi's **Power Spring 4/4S** a recommended tagalong when attending tradeshows and events. Alternately, recharging solutions that serve myriad mobile devices such as the **ZAGGsparq 2.0** or **Motorola 89442N P793 Portable Power Pod** can also provide instant relief for ailing cell phones, tablet PCs and digital cameras. Growingly aware of road warriors' needs, manufacturers are also starting to introduce new smartphones like the **Droid Razr Maxx** that offer 20+ hours of talk time. Buy one, and you can skip paying for additional juice-extending accessories.

Document Printing, Scanning and Signatures – Want to print contracts or invoices straight from your iPad, or your Apple or Android handset? Downloadable apps **PrintCentral Pro** and **Print n Share Pro** let you send document, email or shipping label reproduction requests directly to WiFi printers or office networks via wireless or 3G connections. If a quick signature's all that's needed, document signing and sharing apps like **Sign It!**, **EasySign**, **YouSendIt** can let you ink the deal right from the palm of your hand. Prefer going paperless, or not risking losing meeting notes and invoices in transit between appointments? Portable solutions such as **Scanner Pro**, **Genius Scan** and **CamScanner**, which transform your phone or tablet into a mobile scanner, may also prove a handy upgrade.

File Storage, Sharing and Archival – Kiss accidentally leaving crucial reports or data behind goodbye with cloud file storage and sharing services **Dropbox**, **Box**, **Amazon Cloud Drive** and **SkyDrive**, many of which offer downloadable apps for access via Web or mobile device. Should you need to access your Mac or PC desktop while traveling, a wealth of options including **TeamViewer**, **SplashTop Remote**, **JumpDesktop**, **Remote Desktop Client** and **Wyse PocketCloud** can aid absent-minded entrepreneurs too. Likewise, by letting you upload PowerPoint presentations, slideshows and videos online for on-demand viewing via laptops and tablets, services like **SlideShare**, **SlideShark** and **MightyMeeting** can save forgetful field representatives' jobs.

Task Planning, To-Dos and Organization – Are colleagues constantly bombarding you with useful websites, articles, factoids and business ideas? Record actionable data and items of interest before they go in one ear and out the other with virtual organizer services **Springpad**, **Evernote**, **Catch** and **reQall**, which let you save and catalogue collections of related information including web pages, photos, project checklists and more. Similarly, programs such as **OmniFocus**, **LeaderTask**, **Task PRO**, **Things** and **Toodledo** can make effective substitutes for a personal assistant. All let harried execs plot to-do lists and organize daily schedules.

Travel, Communications and Location-Based Services – Keep up with sudden flight delays, gate changes or shifting itineraries with the **Flight Track Pro** app, a favorite of modern road warriors for its reliable alerts and updates. A helpful complement for travelers, **AroundMe** can track your position and point you towards nearby restaurants, gas stations, hospitals or taxi stands in a pinch as well. Managing expenses is simple too with programs such as **XpenseTracker** and **Expense Tablet** for iOS devices, while portable invoicing solutions **Omni Invoice** and **Invoice2go** let you send quotes and invoices virtually anywhere. Private social network **Neer**, which displays your location to approved contacts, can additionally assist with tracking down missing colleagues or setting area-activated alerts, e.g. shopping lists that appear when you visit Office Depot. Finally, if you're headed out for a conference, consider packing cross-platform text messaging application **WhatsApp** as well. It lets teams send texts, photos and videos for free between varying types of smartphone (BlackBerry, iOS, Android, Nokia), or enjoy group chat features on-demand.

So much for ever watching the best-laid plans short circuit again…

 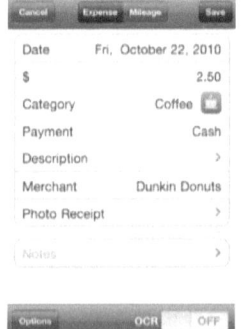

Many free and paid downloadable apps can make doing business easier.

Chapter 21
5 WAYS THE NEW IPAD BENEFITS BUSINESS

S itting somewhere in the murky no man's land between smartphones and traditional laptops, and retailing for a hefty $499 minimum, Apple's new iPad still remains a large question mark from a small business owner's standpoint. While some ambitious entrepreneurs have found ways to make the tablet PC work for their particular enterprise and vertical, others continue to wonder why they should toss their trusty old notebook. Looking for an excuse to add one of these must-see devices to your own IT budget? Here are five ways the new iPad can potentially help you add to the bottom line – and enjoy added personal benefits like the cutting-edge digital publishing, streaming audio/video and game playing capabilities it offers on your next business trip.

1 Product and Video Demonstrations – Despite its lack of Flash support (admittedly less of a future worry given Adobe's decision to throw the platform under the bus), the new iPad's Internet-connected access, touchscreen interface and organic Web surfing experience make it an excellent way to demonstrate online products and services. Businesses that rely on video to tell their story (via reels, testimonials, commercial spots, product demonstrations and more) will also find the gadget's dazzling 9.7-inch display a great method to get the point across, as the new iPad supports video recording and videoconferencing. As a multi-function device backed by thousands of apps, it's further possible to jump between slideshow presentations and pulling up online traffic stats on-demand, making it a solid all-purpose solution when screening examples for retailers, trade partners and prospective clients alike.

2 Endless Functionality – Arguably the gizmo's greatest strength – beyond its powerful A5X processor, quad-core 3D graphics capabilities, breezy 4G LTE download speeds, and user-friendly font-end – is its massive level of support from the third-party software development community. From mobile invoicing and customer relationship management programs to apps that let you track mileage and monitor flight statuses in real-time, a legion of bedroom coders continue to push the device further than even its creators ever imagined. A few quick software purchases and downloads is all it takes to transform the new iPad into a portable translator, inventory management system, voice recorder and more. Buy one, and you may never need another gadget again.

3 Access to Digital Publishing – Via a range of software solutions from the iBooks app to Kindle suite and support for the ePub format, the iPad puts a massive library of publications at your fingertips. Whether you're looking to parse the pages of *USA Today*, read up on *How Companies Win* or enjoy immediate access to a full spate of corporate training manuals, it makes a much more ergonomic, practical and transportable solution than traditional carrying methods. Added bonuses include massive cost-savings, less waste and fewer shipping charges for all parties involved. Think of it as your very own personal digital newsstand.

4 Note-Taking Options – Allowing users to jot down notes on command, scribble out detailed technical sketches or simply dictate important memos, the new iPad may prove a lifesaver for executives who feel overwhelmed by today's incoming torrent of information. Using built-in features and downloadable apps, it's possible to more effectively manage one's calendar, quickly spot holes in your schedule at a glance and **even remember what to pick up on your next trip to Office Depot**. The closest many entrepreneurs will ever come to having a personal assistant, it can oftentimes prove just as handy in terms of keeping you from drowning under a sea of daily minutiae.

5 Constant Connectivity – No matter if you choose to access online functions through a wireless hotspot or 4G LTE high-speed cellular network, the new iPad lets you keep up with email, monitor emerging trends around the Web and stay abreast of breaking headlines. Using the device, you can stay in touch with colleagues across time zones and continents, remain on top of shifting stock prices and catch topics relevant to your industry as they storm the international newswires. Those who've been holding out on purchasing a smartphone, given usage patterns that lean more towards data-intensive tasks than reams of conference calls, may find it a welcome alternative.

Is the iPad 2 Right for You?

Though it's no longer the newest model fresh off Apple's factory line, the iPad 2 remains a clear market leader in tablet PC computing, and offers several key benefits beyond its predecessor for those looking to shop the company's back catalogue.

In addition to dual cameras for casual videoconferencing or high-definition video recording and a slimmer form factor that's 33% thinner and 15% lighter than the original iPad (also worth picking up from online resellers), it also packs roughly twice as much computing muscle. But while additions like a speedier 1GHz dual-core A5 processor and graphics chip that pumps out polygons nine times faster sound good on paper, the question remains. Priced starting at $399 for 16GB WiFi units and $529 for 64GB WiFi and 3G-enabled editions, and now competing with dozens of rivals from the Asus Transformer Prime to the Samsung Galaxy Tab, is it right for your business?

Intriguingly, the answer may lie not in what the second-generation iPad offers, but rather what it instead lacks.

Currently incompatible with high-speed 4G networks like the new iPad, the device may not download from the Internet fast enough to keep up with an increasingly mobile workforce's needs going forward. This can be problematic, especially when dealing with large files such as multimedia content or satellite imagery. The issue is likely to become further pronounced in coming months, as increasingly more advanced apps continue to grow in size, scope and depth with each passing day. But if you're not dealing with large volumes of data or simply using the iPad 2 for everyday tasks such as surfing the Web and sending email, current 3G speeds may be more than enough. From streaming video to sharing documents and interfacing with online programs, it's up to all but the most arduous routine tasks.

Flash web browsing, which allows for richer animations and interactivity on certain sites, is also missing, though Adobe's decision to abandon the format for mobile devices does make it less of a pressing concern going forward. Still, small business owners whose online headquarters utilize this technology, or rely on it for product demonstrations, may prefer to choose compatible tablets based on the Android operating system instead. These devices – which support Android Honeycomb, an interface specifically optimized for tablet PCs, or successor "Ice Cream Sandwich" (Android 4.0) – could offer those who put speed and multitasking first a better alternative as well. Running on the evolutionary, not revolutionary, iOS 5 operating system, the iPad 2 does provide the benefit of streamlined Web browsing and use of one's iPhone as a WiFi hotspot, however.

Offering the same 9.7-inch touchscreen as the original iPad, rather than a glare-resistant option or crisper monitor like the iPhone 4S and new iPad's Retina display, you may also prefer competing units' smaller, larger or more adaptable screens, priced accordingly. From crisper resolution to more visual real estate, it's worth considering all options, given slate computers' growing emphasis on digital publishing, eye-catching multimedia and visually-oriented productivity apps. Though capable of recording 720p video on its rear-facing camera, and powering video calls between Mac, iPhone 4 and iPod Touch owners using the FaceTime app, the iPad 2 makes a poor digital camera replacement too. Still shots are pegged at around 0.92MP, which puts their quality on par with last century's outings, making the device a hard sell for those who enjoy a good photo op or power personal communicators.

Other downsides include a lack of SD Memory Card and mini-USB ports, which would allow for easy, affordable storage expansion. Cutting-edge features such as near field communications (NFC) technology, which lets you pay bills or exchange info electronically with posters, vending machines and everyday objects embedded with special chips, are also missing. Battery life further tops out at 10 hours, more than the average notebook PC, but less than new laptops like the ThinkPad T420 and HP EliteBook 8460p, which promise 30+ hours of juice. Still, while not the most cost-conscious or even universal laptop replacement, the iPad 2 does stand head over shoulders above competing tablets, and notebook PCs, in certain areas.

Incredibly portable, versatile and a beauty to behold, it remains one of the easiest portable computing options to travel with, and most visually arresting to conduct presentations or product demos on. Support for over 140,000 dedicated apps also provides the gadget with unmatched versatility, allowing it to double as a mobile invoice tracker, inventory replenishment solution or even foreign language translator on command. Among the easiest and most enjoyable units to browse digital publications on, the iPad 2 also makes a natural fit for sharing and skimming corporate communications, continuing education and training materials.

But perhaps best of all are the doors the device now opens in terms of digital communications. Enabling face-to-face interaction through new videoconferencing features, it allows you to enjoy more personal relationships with clients and colleagues, and conduct meetings virtually anytime, anywhere. Providing a portable window onto your world, it also lets entrepreneurs and working professionals more effortlessly collaborate and share ideas with coworkers the globe over. Road warriors will further appreciate added benefits, i.e. the ability to personally say goodnight to their spouse or tuck children into bed, despite being an ocean or several time zones away. Aspiring directors or website owners hungry for content can also take advantage of high-definition video recording features to capture video diaries, customer testimonials and product demos on-demand.

Most important of all, coupled with unprecedented support from the third-party software development community, the iPad 2 and its feature set continue to grow at a blistering clip. While the tablet PC may seem primarily focused on entertainment and leisurely escapes, it would be a mistake to judge the unit at face value alone. Placed in the hands of enterprising coders determined to push the device and its capabilities to the limit, realize: Business owners may find it more than a match for their needs, and potentially, even a better value than its newer, shinier sibling.

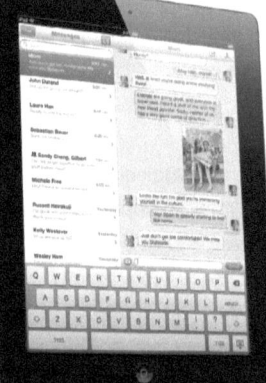

Chapter 22
10 TIPS FOR ONLINE AND HIGH-TECH SECURITY

Technology continues to be a boon for entrepreneurs, offering increased mobility, productivity and cost-saving efficiencies at shrinking expense. But useful as modern innovations such as smartphones, tablet PCs and cloud computing are to small businesses, they also present growing security concerns. Following are 10 safety tips to help you guard against high-tech failure:

1 **Protect with Passwords** – This may seem like a no-brainer, but many cyber attacks succeed precisely because of weak password protocols. Access to all equipment, wireless networks and sensitive data should always be guarded with unique user names and passwords keyed to specific individuals. The strongest passwords contain numbers, letters and symbols, and aren't based on commonplace words, standard dictionary terms or easy-to-guess dates such as birthdays or anniversaries. Each user should further have a unique password wherever it appears on a device or network. If you absolutely, positively can't avoid living without a master document containing all user passcodes, be certain to encrypt it with its own passcode and store it in a secure place.

2 **Design Safe Systems** – Reduce exposure to hackers and thieves by limiting access to your technology infrastructure. Minimize points of failure by eliminating unnecessary access to hardware and software, and restricting individual users' and systems' privileges only to needed equipment and programs. Whenever possible, minimize the scope of potential damage to your networks by using a unique set of email addresses, logins, servers and domain names for each user, work group or department as well.

3 **Conduct Screening and Background Checks** – While rogue hackers get most of the press, the majority of unauthorized intrusions occur from inside network firewalls. Screen all prospective employees from the mailroom to the executive suite. Beyond simply calling references, be certain to research their credibility as well. An initial trial period, during which access to sensitive data is either prohibited or limited, is also recommended. Login information and system usage should further be logged and monitored for suspicious activity as well.

4 **Provide Basic Training** – Countless security breaches inevitably occur as a result of human error or carelessness. But educating associates on the risks of skipping precautionary steps, and building a corporate culture that prizes preventative measures, can help mitigate risk.

From basic document disposal procedures to established protocols for handling lost passwords, all security measures should be second-nature to members of your organization.

5 **Avoid Unknown Email Attachments** – Never, ever click on unsolicited email attachments, which can contain viruses, Trojans or computer worms. Before opening them, always contact the sender to confirm message contents. If you're unfamiliar with the source, it's always best to err on the side of caution.

6 **Hang Up and Call Back** – So-called "social engineers," or cons with a gift for gab, often prey on unsuspecting victims by pretending to be someone they're not. If a purported representative from the bank or strategic partner seeking sensitive data phones, always end the call and hang up. Then dial your direct contact at that organization, or one of its publicly listed numbers to confirm if the call was legitimate. Never try to verify suspicious calls with a number provided by the caller.

Password protection is a must in today's digital world

7 **Think Before You Click** – Phishing scams operate by sending innocent-looking emails from apparently trusted sources asking for usernames, passwords or personal information. Some scam artists even create fake Web sites that encourage potential victims from inputting the data themselves. Rather than activate suspicious links or reply to emails with billing or address information, instead find the corresponding company's website online and surf there directly, or pick up the phone and call before providing such info or clicking on suspicious links.

8 **Utilize a Virus Scanner and Keep All Software Up-to-Date** – Whether working at home or across an office network, it pays to install basic virus scanning capability on your PC. Many network providers now offer such applications for free. Keeping software of all types up to date is also imperative, including scheduling regular downloads of security updates, which help guard against new viruses and variations of old threats.

9 **Keep Sensitive Data Out of the Cloud** – Cloud computing offers businesses many benefits from remote storage and archival to simultaneous project synchronization across multiple desktops. But such services could also pose additional threats as data is housed on remote servers operated by third parties who may have their own security issues. For everyday tasks, such solutions can be a boon, and provide great advantages if you're working with lower-priority data. With many cloud-based services still in their infancy though, it's prudent for now to keep your most confidential information on your own networks.

10 **Stay Paranoid** – Shred everything, including documents with corporate names, addresses and others information, including the logos of vendors and banks you deal with. Never leave sensitive reports out on your desk or otherwise accessible for any sustained period of time, let alone overnight. Change passwords regularly and often, especially if you've shared them with an associate. It may seem obsessive, but a healthy dose of paranoia could prevent a major data breach.

The average cost to an organization to recover from a data breach hovers at around $6.75 million, according to Javelin Strategy & Research, not counting damages to relationships or your reputation. So remember: You can never be too careful. No matter how much things change, being proactive still remains the best solution for avoiding falling victim to security failures and other common IT issues.

Chapter 23
STORAGE SOLUTIONS:
PROTECT DATA FROM CATASTROPHIC FAILURE

While allocating additional funds for information archival may seem like a frivolous expense, especially for a well-oiled small business, there are two salient points to consider when debating the possible costs associated with data backup.

One: Preventative measures are far more affordable and far-reaching than reactive solutions, with any up-front cash outlay paling in comparison to what you'd spend attempting to recover crucial files following a catastrophic system failure. And two, should costs seem unreasonable, always keep the following in mind. In the early days of home computing, PC owners paid upwards of a $1 per MB of disk space, hardly enough to hold even a single high-resolution photo by today's standards. As such, you're getting the bargain of the century by comparison, especially considering how much file recovery issues can ultimately cost in terms of delays, downtime and loss of productivity and customer goodwill.

Cheerfully, with storage prices plummeting in recent years, it's easy for small business owners to tack on added virtual safeguards to any enterprise without investing in racks of expensive servers or high-end digital archival solutions. Courtesy of a range of new plug and play external and portable hard drive options, your data can easily be copied and backed up regularly, preventing against power surges and file corruption, as well as travel wherever you do. To wit, the following selections all make sound investments in your company's future, allowing you to quickly and painlessly resurrect vital transaction records, billing details and customer info in the event of desktop meltdown.

But first, a word of advice: For most basic purposes including business travel and making duplicates of temporary files for quick transfer between computers, a USB Flash Drive will suffice. Also known as "USB keys" or "thumb drives," these storage options – which plug right into your Mac or PC's USB port and require no additional software or cables – are among the most portable and versatile archival solutions available. Roughly the same dimensions as a money clip or stick of gum, options generally range in scope from 2GB ($5 and up) to 64GB ($69 and up) of available storage space. (You can also now find 128GB and 256GB models available from manufacturers such as Kingston; they will cost you in the $200-300 range.)

Effectively functioning as today's floppy disk equivalent, dozens of choices are available courtesy of vendors such as SanDisk, PNY and Corsair, so be sure to shop around. In most cases, you'll be able to get away with buying models of 4GB to 8GB or less in size, unless working with larger files such as digital video or music. Available in countless shapes and varieties (including some units modeled to look like rubber ducks or hidden inside watches and pens), it should be relatively easy and inexpensive to find a model that suits your needs.

Likewise, a number of Internet-based storage options such as **Google Drive**, **Amazon**

<u>Cloud Drive</u>, <u>Windows Live SkyDrive</u>, <u>YouSendIt</u>, <u>Box</u> and <u>Dropbox</u> make it easy to warehouse or transfer large files online. (Many of which don't cost a cent for general, everyday use, with paid service plans typically reserved for bulk usage or businesses that require significant amounts of data archival or transfer.) In certain cases, you'll even be able to share files and collaborate on projects in real-time. It's a feature that those familiar with cloud computing services (which can safely store data on remote servers for access from any Internet-connected device) such as Google Docs and Zoho Suite already enjoy.

Entrepreneurs who need ongoing backup options on a grander scale or prefer a larger physical repository for transportable data are advised to look at external hard drive (HD) options though, with common varieties ranging up to 6TB in size and $90-550 in price. (At least, the kind you're most likely to stumble across at your local retailer – for bigger options, see a specialty vendor or consider ordering online.) For example: Western Digital's MyBook World Edition II makes a suitable choice for the paranoid, with automatic mirrored backup providing ongoing data redundancy as a helpful safeguard. Units, which hold hundreds of thousands of files, songs, videos and photos, also offer the option to wirelessly stream multimedia to Mac, PC or TV, doubling as a hub for digital content. Likewise, key sales presentations and purchase orders can be retrieved over the Internet if accidentally left back at the home office, proving a lifesaver should you forget important files before hitting the road.

Seagate's Replica, offered in 250GB and 500GB sizes, also provides continuous automated data backup on a smaller scale. Clickfree similarly offers a number of equally roadworthy and recommendable backup solutions starting at 120GB capacities with credit card-sized Traveler models beginning at 16GB in size as well. As such, simply plug and play to enjoy consistency amongst all your files, with up-to-date saves of all data stored without prompting, allowing you to easily restore a single hard drive or recover your entire computer from a fatal crash.

Several other manufacturers also offer cheaper alternatives ($80-$160) which require a little manual effort (e.g., remembering to drag and drop copies of important files with some degree of regularity) on your part. See Iomega's eGo line, with both rugged and portable options that guard against drops from roughly four feet in height and desktop solutions offered. There's even a 1TB BlackBelt edition that ups drop-proof capabilities to 7 feet in height and provides online file backup options. Likewise, Seagate's carry-on ready FreeAgent GoFlex and Desk models also make welcome choices. But with external HD storage technology largely standardized and cost-affordable, you'll find plenty of great alternatives from countless additional manufacturers like LaCie and Hitachi.

The bottom line for entrepreneurs: You don't have to pay much for a little peace of mind, thanks to an unparalleled range of off-the-shelf solutions. Think proactively, and you can still save your business' precious data, or carry crucial files along on the road, without having to blow a small fortune on custom network storage devices or worse.

Best Cloud Storage Services for Business

Whatever size your business happens to be, you can always benefit from centralized Web-accessible storage. Cloud storage solutions are particularly helpful to businesses with virtual workforces or employees who travel frequently, given the ability to remotely save, organize, and share files – which is quickly becoming essential to today's entrepreneur. Cloud storage comes in a variety of sizes to meet the needs of an equally broad range of businesses. As your enterprise (and budget) grows, you can always upgrade to new levels of storage and/or new storage services that will meet your changing needs. Here are some of the best storage services for businesses today.

DropBox – Although Dropbox offers less free storage than other options, it is ideal for users with multiple computers or mobile devices and is simple to use. Additionally, Dropbox tracks all changes made to uploaded documents and allows users to use older versions if necessary. It offers 2GB of free storage and pricing plans including $10 per month for 50GB of storage or $20 per month for 100GB of storage.

Amazon Cloud Drive – The service works with any type of file, and is especially good at streaming music to any computer or Android-based device. It provides 5GB of free storage, with additional storage priced at $1 per GB per month (e.g. 20GB costs $20, 50GB costs $50, etc.), with a maximum of 1TB of space available ($1,000 per month).

Box – Gives 5GB of free storage, with the ability to upload files of up to 25MB in size each, to individual users per month. A 25GB/1GB per month individual option is available for $10 and a 50GB/1GB per month option available for $20 as well. For business plans (1000GB of storage and 2GB file uploads), Box charges $15 per user per month. An unlimited "enterprise" account is available too (call for pricing).

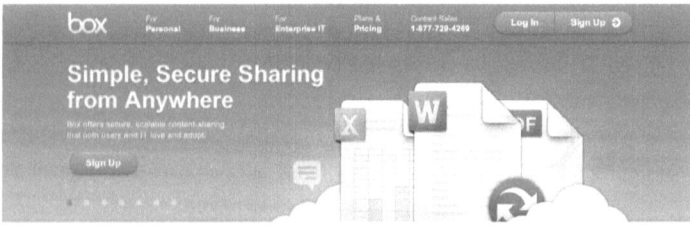

Windows Live SkyDrive – One of the best 100% free services available, with files easily uploaded, organized and shared to it. SkyDrive also offers integrated support for the Microsoft Web Apps suite. You get a maximum 25GB of free storage – an upside or down, depending on your needs.

Chapter 24
PROTECTING YOUR BUSINESS FROM IDENTITY THEFT

A Harvard University honors graduate and head of a thriving startup, 10 years ago entrepreneur John Sileo was by all rights a smashing success. But then his entire life changed with a knock. At the door: An investigator for the Denver district attorney's office, alleging that Sileo had stolen $300,000 from his clients.

Like hundreds of fellow businesses and government agencies each year, he'd become the victim of identity theft. But in this case, for the second time – and courtesy of his former business partner. More frightening still, as the *Privacy Means Profit* author and professional speaker warns, if it can happen to him, it can happen to anyone—especially you and your business.

"Even the most seemingly innocent data such as names, addresses and employment histories are at risk," Sileo cautions. "While the media likes to talk about high-tech methods of data theft, the reality is that most crimes occur the same way they did 10 years ago–through human error. Every office is filled with potential hazards, from unshredded reports to computers left logged into private networks and sensitive documents that somehow end up in the trash."

Having been victimized through both his own negligence (forgetting to destroy personal mortgage documents) and naiveté (allowing an untrustworthy associate to manage his firm's accounting), Sileo can't stress the importance of caution enough. Because even when justice is served, as in the case of his onetime partner, who went to jail for just 18 days and has since returned to private commerce, it's often scant compensation for the loss of your reputation or customers' trust.

Hazards in the Workplace

Piles of sensitive data can provide a potential windfall to crooks, with prime targets including bank account numbers and credit card info. But other less obvious, yet just as juicy plums can also include customer data or employee records. Valuable intellectual capital ranging from your family restaurant's secret recipe to firm's client list acts like a beacon to criminal elements as well.

Unfortunately, points of vulnerability are vast and manifold. Everything from unshredded financial statements to out-of-date computer virus scanning programs or stolen laptops that have been left unguarded by software encryption can present a possible problem area. Nor is even your own desk safe anymore, as documents left on it overnight may fall victim to an unscrupulous member of the cleaning staff.

All it takes is a few scant crumbs of information to attract predators. Because once a scent's obtained, they can quickly use this data to sniff out other, more sensitive details. Armed with just names, addresses and phone numbers, thieves can often con or compute their way into enough information to register credit cards, run up bills and otherwise wreak havoc in your company's name.

Worse, such incidents can prove pricey setbacks. The average cost to an organization to recover from a data breach hovers at $6.75 million, with more than $54 billion in total damages racked up in 2009 alone, according to Javelin Strategy & Research. But that doesn't count loss of productivity, customer goodwill or brand equity. Just ask Sileo, who spent more than 500 hours recovering his good name, suffered untold humiliation, had to rebuild his entire credit history and lost his family's 40-year-old business personally cleaning up a similar mess.

Sensitive data should always be properly safeguarded and/or disposed of through shredding.

Smart Steps for Prevention

Thankfully, "an ounce of prevention far outweighs a pound of cure," he says, recommending several strategies to guard against data loss:

■ Conducting simple employee background screenings and reference checks makes a good starting point, he advises, including researching the credibility of supporting references themselves.

■ All computer equipment that your business uses, including hard drives, laptops, USB keys and smartphones should be encrypted and equipped with a password as well.

■ But most vital, Sileo says, is creating a corporate culture that supports preventative measures. Not only should employees be offered basic training that clearly illustrates the risks of not taking regular precautionary steps. Company policy should also make it simple and convenient to take part in the process.

■ "Part of the problem's due to ignorance, some of it stupidity, and you also have to throw in some apathy and lack of awareness," Sileo sighs. "People assume that they can protect their systems."

But with inside theft (e.g., a carefully bribed janitor), dodgy software protection (beware unsecured WiFi hotspots, which hackers can monitor) and clever cons (a healthy fear of unsolicited emails/calls helps) growingly omnipresent dangers, consider. As the commercial sector moves more toward wireless solutions ("never use the same password for multiple purposes") and cloud computing ("beware trading redundancy and scalability for control of your data"), you can never be too paranoid.

Not that guarding against identity theft needs to be an expensive or even time-consuming proposition. "Just think like a spy," chuckles Sileo. "It never hurts to maintain a healthy sense of suspicion, or plan ahead."

Chapter 25
7 WAYS TO MAKE A SMALL BUSINESS LOOK BIG

Current lack of budget, manpower and resources notwithstanding, you know that your bedroom startup has what it takes to compete with today's industry leaders. But regardless of whether your customers are everyday shoppers or corporate clients, it's vital to let them know as well by looking the part.

First impressions being what they are, dressing for success isn't just imperative. It also directly influences brand perception. Thankfully, a number of affordable, cost-effective technology solutions let even the smallest business appear much bigger. Looking to compete with larger companies sans additional hires or assuming crippling overhead? The following apps and high-tech online services can help.

1 Design a Killer Website – Need a professional-looking website, but lack the time, cash and technical know-how to get started? Try **Onepager**, which lets beginners build an attractive online presence in minutes. Using an intuitive point-and-click interface, just insert your company name, tagline and body text into preexisting templates, then add photos and visual styling. Further options allow for insertion of newsletter signups, service rundowns, social media links and contact information, including painless domain name registration. Note that providers like **Intuit**, **1&1**, **Yahoo!** and **Squarespace** also offer painless off-the-shelf solutions.

2 Hire a Virtual Secretary – Rather than ask your poor, frazzled spouse to field calls, instead setup a toll-free number with a customized receptionist that forwards to your cell or home office. Services like **eVoice**, **Grasshopper** and **FreedomNumber** can provide local or long-distance extensions with automated attendant greetings and extensions, which adds to the professionalism of your company's image. Others such as **Phone.com**, **Onebox** and **RingCentral** even offer unlimited calling and faxing, and/or contract-free plans. Fax to email services with companion apps such as **eFax** may also prove a handy solution for receiving documents to go.

3 Host Conference Calls – Three-way calling's for the birds. To setup toll-free extensions for group conversation, try **SimpleTollFree**'s service, which also allows for optional audio recording as well. (The catch: You pay by the minute.) Additional services including **FreeConference**, **Free Conference Calling** and **Rondee** can also provide lines on-demand without prior reservations. International callers may want to try alternatives **PowWowNow** or **No Cost Conference** as well.

4 **Teleconference or Telecommute** – Popular service Skype remains a top way to place video calls free, even in the professional world. (Just remember to clean up and decorate your desk before pointing a webcam at it.) But rivals like ooVoo, FaceFlow and Fring may also prove a useful solution for group chats, while services like FaceTime and Tango provide solutions that extend beyond the desktop to mobile devices as well. Conveniently, all offer a useful way to stay in touch with virtualized colleagues working from their basements to boot.

5 **Cancel Your Lease on Office Space** – Don't need physical retail locations, operate in multiple cities or prefer keeping a desk strictly on a part-time basis? Besides providing professional call answering services and local addresses for package receipt, Regus also rents access to business lounges, conference rooms, office space and equipment at multiple locations on-demand. Rival Alliance Virtual Offices can also supply receptionists, handle delivery receipts and offer temporary office space the world over. If you're a freelancer or startup needing more flexible or longer-term space, alternatives like co-ops and shared offices may be preferable. Intelligent Office, Regent Business Centers and Green Desk can help locate suitable solutions.

6 **Outsource Graphic and Logo Design** – First-rate visual assets often cost a bundle, unless you're friends with a graphic designer. Not so with Crowdspring, which lets you set a budget and project description, then relax while creative types compete to submit potential entries for logos, letterhead and web designs. Fellow services 99Designs and DesignCrowd, which let you run similar contests and provide feedback on submissions, also help steer artists towards creating your dream business card or product labels. The net result with all: You purchase your favorite work from interpretations by dozens of artists.

7 **Create an Online Store** – One way to make money on the Internet: Add an attractive, flexible online storefront that's brimming with must-have goods. Multiple options from Yahoo! and Goodsie to Shopify, Volusion and BigCommerce can help by offering both basic solutions that require minimal to no programming and more sophisticated virtual bazaars. Note that while it's tempting to go big on features and selection here, it often pays to keep things simple. Start by staying focused on practicality, convenience and popular high-margin goods, then expand organically, rather than risking overcomplicating your user interface or overwhelming shoppers with too many choices.

Chapter 26
8 REASONS TO FIRE YOUR PERSONAL ASSISTANT

C all them executive assistants, personal assistants or just handy lifesavers – either way, their services don't come cheap. But then again, neither does your time, for that matter. Thankfully for those who can't afford someone to book appointments or manage their topsy-turvy schedule, a number of apps promise to offer similar functionality.

Download or sign-up for any of the following software programs or online Web services, and you'll be better equipped to plot to-do lists, juggle appointments and handle project management. Just don't let your PA catch wind of them, or they may start polishing their resume.

1 **Evernote** – Lets you tame professional life's clutter by taking virtual memos on-demand. Able to store text, photos and voice recordings, Evernote allows you to dictate notes (and add location tagging), store articles, snap pictures and automatically synchronize updates across your computer, smartphone and tablet. Keyword, tag and text searches aid with information retrieval.

2 **reQall** – Helps you juggle daily to-do lists, save sudden flashes of inspiration, or remember errands to run by letting you record notes via voice, text, email or instant message. Once jotted down, you can organize action items by location, date or time, and even assign tags, categories, keywords and locations for easier cataloguing. Programmable reminders even tell you what to do right on time, or on the spot.

3 **CardMunch** – LinkedIn's app transforms business cards into virtual contacts, so you can store and share them on mobile devices, and quickly pull up associates' online profiles. Shockingly, instead of high-tech scanning solutions, images are actually transcribed by real humans, ensuring optimum accuracy for your address book.

4 **OmniFocus** – More expensive than most apps, this time management suite ultimately saves users money by making plotting daily agendas simpler. Capable of organizing tasks by groups, contexts, tools, locations and resources, it helps you keep tabs on ongoing engagements and prioritize to-do lists. Support for synchronizing between multiple devices proves a welcome addition.

5 **Remember the Milk** – Capable of integrating with mobile, web and desktop apps (Gmail, Google Calendar, Outlook, iCal, etc.) and synchronizing across multiple devices, this popular list-making utility keeps you from forgetting tasks or outstanding action items. Options to organize deliverables by priority or due date prove especially handy, with optional reminders (email, SMS, instant messenger, etc.), time estimates and task grouping functions also welcome additions.

6 **Gist** – Organize, manage and update your ever-growing crush of contacts in a single location with minimal fuss. Capable of importing email, phone and address data from multiple sources (inbox, social network, smartphone, etc), the program makes keeping up with acquaintances' constantly-shifting details painless. Options to view colleagues' running Facebook and Twitter feeds without exiting are just an added bonus.

7 **Week Calendar** – Goes beyond the iPhone's basic calendar app to provide weekly overviews (day-, month-, year- and agenda-based overviews available as well) with support for extensive customization. Providing a visually attractive and feature-rich approach for drag-and-drop or cut-and-paste plotting, color-coding and organization of events, OCD types will appreciate its multitude of extras. From batch editing to options to link contacts to creations, the program doesn't skip on options.

8 **AwesomeNote (+Todo)** – A graphical organizer that lets you save notes, build to-do lists, and assign color-coded tags, fonts, icons and backgrounds to creations for more effective cataloguing and categorization. From travel itineraries to conference schedules, you can plot all on a nicely-appointed calendar, and add photos, maps, sketches and assorted images. Folders can also be created and assigned unique passwords for faster grouping and storage.

Don't forget to take advantage of AwesomeNote (+Todo) and other powerful organization apps—time is a valuable commodity for the small business owner.

ABOUT SCOTT STEINBERG

AUTHOR | SPEAKER | CONSULTANT | SPOKESPERSON | EXPERT WITNESS

Small business expert **Scott Steinberg** is the creator of The Business Expert's Guidebook series and one of today's most celebrated **strategic consultants**, **keynote speakers**, **corporate spokespersons** and **expert witnesses**. The host of video show *Business Expert: Small Business Tips, Trends and Advice* and a popular business speaker, he regularly appears as an on-air authority for all major TV networks including ABC, CBS, FOX, NBC and CNN.

Hailed as a leading business and technology expert by top publications from *The Wall St. Journal* to *BusinessWeek* and NPR, he's covered the field for 400+ outlets from *The New York Times* to *Inc.* and *Entrepreneur*. The CEO of business consulting and product testing firm **TechSavvy Global**, Steinberg is also a nationally-syndicated small business columnist and noted entrepreneur who's founded and sold multiple firms. A well-known business keynote guest speaker and media figure, he additionally hosts several popular video shows including *Tech Industry Insider, Gear Up* and *Game Theory*. The author of over half a dozen books on business, marketing and technology, his companies publish software, websites, magazines, films and more.

As a top motivational and **youth speaker**, he's presented and hosted events for governments, Fortune 500 corporations and industry trade groups worldwide. Steinberg further aids industry leaders, attorneys and investors with business strategy consulting, expert witness testimony and market analysis. Between public speaking ops, instructional videos, articles and podcasts, he remains one of the industry's most outspoken DIY evangelists and advocates for **continuing education**.

For more info, see **www.ASmallBusinessExpert.com**.